SECOND EDITION

LOGIC

WITHOUT ALL OF THE **LOGIC**

AN INTRODUCTION WITH EXERCISES

Bradley Wakefield

Macomb Community College

Kendall Hunt
publishing company

www.kendallhunt.com
Send all inquiries to:
4050 Westmark Drive
Dubuque, IA 52004-1840

ISBN 978-1-5249-8799-2

Published in the United States of America.

PREFACE

Logic Without All of the Logic: An Introduction with Exercises is a textbook designed for introductory logic courses. The text is meant to be completed from front to back cover in only one semester. This introduction to the classical logic is meant to familiarize the student with some of the basic concepts of logic. Although many of these topics are up for debate, especially amongst philosophers, it is not the purpose of this book. Before we can reasonably doubt or scrutinize the concepts of logic, we must first get acquainted with the concepts. In this sense, the text should be viewed as an elementary approach to studying logic and not the substantive work in the philosophy of logic. Many of the themes in this book may appear commonsensical and other parts less intuitive. In a broad sense, this textbook teaches you how to construct and evaluate arguments in a clear and concise way. Arguments are used in many different fields such as: political theory, sociology, physical sciences, medical science, mathematics, business, history, art, ordinary conversations, etc. So, the benefits of this course material are incalculable.

Ordinary language is often informal or colloquial and does not require the precision that you will find in classical logic. For example, we ordinarily think of the word "some" to mean part of a whole. Thus, when I use words like "some are not" that would encompass the other half of the whole. However, we need to depart from the colloquial usage of these terms and refine and adhere to the meanings found in classical logic. In mathematics, you must abide by a set of rules and/or principles to derive necessary truths. Classical logic functions in a very similar way. Most of this textbook is helping you establish the rules and/or principles of classical logic. Thus, you will see a common theme in this textbook of truth preserving rules and/or principles.

Finally, this textbook is written to help you understand the basic components of classical logic to either aid you in other disciplines or to advance your studies in logic as a whole (three-valued logic, fuzzy logic, modal logic, predicate logic, logical systems, probability theory, etc.). After completion of this text, you will be prepared to enter an advanced symbolic logic course.

The explanations and exercises are short and concise. I decided to not include long-winded definitions and explanations for the simple fact that it is superfluous in an introductory text. I have attempted to reduce the complexities of classical logic down to simple digestible parts. However, due to the fact that we are all fallible, it is certainly possible that there are some mistakes contained in this work. Thus, revisions or contributions are always welcomed.

CONTENT LAYOUT

This textbook is divided into five sections. The sections are as follows:

- Introduction and aim of the book
- Basic Concepts and Terms
- Argument Recognition
- Informal Logic
- Formal Logic

The textbook is written in such a way that we will progress one section at a time, whereas each section will build upon the previous sections. Although the specific logic course that you are taking may not be cumulative, the content of this book is rather cumulative. So, if you do not fully understand a particular section, then it may hamper your ability to move onto further sections of the text. The exercises are meant to engage you in the course material and to serve as practice in order to perfect your understanding of the concepts of classical logic.

You will notice that in each homework section there are a few problems with an asterisk next to it. Those questions have their answers in the end of the text. You may use those answers to verify that you are, in fact, understanding how to complete the practice problems.

ACKNOWLEDGEMENTS

I am truly grateful to my colleagues, friends, and family who have supported me during this process. Without them, I would not have been able to complete this book. Their patience, contributions, corrections, revisions, and general enthusiasm have allowed me to keep my focus and ultimately complete this book.

I am also thankful for the help and support from Kendall Hunt Publishing. Torrie Johnson, Tracey D. DeBrincat, and Rachel Guhin were always available to answer any questions or problems that I encountered. Their constant encouragement kept me optimistic about this project.

I would like to recognize some of my colleagues and former professors who helped show me the intellectually stimulating process of philosophy, and more specifically, classical logic. A special thanks to Mark Huston, Schoolcraft College; Margaret Crouch, Eastern Michigan University; Jill Dieterle, Eastern Michigan University; Sarah Heidt, Eastern Michigan University; Gregory Novack, Wayne State University; Travis Figg, Wayne State University; Drew Matzke, Wayne State University; Lewis Powell, Wayne State University; James Tierney, Macomb Community College; Theresa Catalano-Reinhardt, Macomb Community College; Dorothy Morosoff, Macomb Community College; Robert Graham, Macomb Community College; Michael Gavin, Macomb Community College; Ryan LeMasters, Schoolcraft College; Jesse Mileo, Schoolcraft College; Daniel Fick, Schoolcraft College; Timothy Kirschenheiter, Wayne State University; Joseph Dunne, University of Michigan-Dearborn; Emily Chudy, Macomb Community College; Stephanie Scott; Jamie Borkowski; and my parents. Lastly, I would like to thank my closest friend and life partner, Meghann Rutherford, who always pushes me to do my best work. Meghann and I have had so many great debates over the years, and I have learned so much from her.

CONTENTS

SECTION I

Introduction

a. The aim of this book

1. The world in which we live is continually changing, growing, progressing, and occasionally moving backward. Since the 1990s, we have lived in what's best known as the *digital age*. We have all of the information right at our fingertips. Any obscure fact about dinosaurs, quarks, deciduous plants, or military weapons is immediately available. It seems as though any fact that you so desire is only a click away. This has made life much more simplified. In the past, our minds were filled with copious amounts of information. Most of which was implanted there from a very young age. In fact, it took a lot of cognitive brain power to store all of that information. Now that we live in the *digital age*, we no longer need to store all of this information in our minds. Our smartphones have become an essential tool in our modern day arsenal. We now have the chance to clear our memory (the hard drive of the mind) of all of those facts about the world, knowing that they are only a click away on our devices. So, the question then becomes, "Where do we direct our cognitive abilities?"

   In the *digital age*, we think that facts are the absolute end-all of every possible dispute. If you give someone a few moments to look up the answer on their phone, then they can solve any debate. Thus, our modern world is fast, loose, and fact driven. I think that there are a few things to say here. First is that we need to establish which facts are true from those that are false. This is not something peculiar to logic because every discipline spends their efforts trying to prove things conclusively. Second, is that we need to recognize that although facts are very significant, they do not always solve many of the great questions that we have. Why is that, do you ask? Well, going back to Ancient Greece, a group of proto-scientific thinkers realized that facts need to be assembled in a very particular sort of way. Some facts, when put together with other facts, allow us to extrapolate further facts. Some facts seem to possess some internal connection to other facts about the world. For example, from the fact that my Netflix app is not loading and says "Connection Error" to another fact that the Hulu app does not have any problems loading allows you to infer that there is not a network error. For if there were some network error, then Hulu would not be able to load. You could immediately surmise that the network is not having any problems by reasoning your way through the other two facts. The fact that there is no network error is evidenced by and only by the fact that Netflix says, "Connection Error" and Hulu does not. Without those two facts, we would not be able to speak on behalf of the functioning or lack thereof the network.

So much of our knowledge is derived from inferences like the example given above. Without having a proper understanding of logic, you will not be able to draw reasonable conclusions about how the world really is. We rely on experience to tell us about the nature of the world. However, we should also recognize that most of the things we know about the world are not directly observed, they are inferred. Direct and first-hand experience only amounts to a tiny section of our edifice of knowledge. That means that in order to gain more knowledge about the world one must be trained how to do so. We are sometimes led to believe that some of the concepts of logic are intuitive or self-evident. However, we must also recognize that this is a short-sighted view of human rationality. Human rationality is a skill that needs the training to do it well. Most mathematical training that you have done is to prepare you for critical thinking. In fact, critical thinking is a fundamental component of every course in higher education. Though critical thinking is an essential part of your education, the training that you have had is somewhat implicit. This book aims to provide an explicit introduction to critical thinking by employing readings, exercises, analogies, and everyday examples to highlight the practical implications.

2. Many of the themes in this book are to show you precisely what not to do. This may strike some as counterintuitive unless I elaborate a bit. We often think that we should strive for the correct answer. In fact, since we were in grade school, we were told that finding the correct answer is the proper motivation for education. Thus, when we were unable to find that answer, the teacher would come along and provide the antidote. When education works in this way, the students are not really learning, in any robust sense. Instead, we need to come to terms with the idea that learning occurs through failure. When we fail, we must, first of all, learn about the failure. Once we understand why the process was mistaken, we then begin to correct our train of thought and find a more appropriate way in which to solve a particular problem.

   For example, suppose you were traveling on the "Oregon Trail," and you encountered a large fork in the road. For the sake of argument let's say that there were six possible options, each of which are taking you in a different direction. We will ask ourselves, "Which direction is the right one?" Now it appears that we have no special insight into the nature of the trail, and it would be completely arbitrary to pick a certain path over another. Prima facie, we do not know which path is going to lead us in the right direction, and which path could lead us to our inevitable death. This example is quite analogous to us right now. We might think we have an idea where we are headed, but this is very unlikely. As little as thirty years ago, we had no idea that people would be fixed to tiny devices right in front of their faces. Rather than fixating on which direction is the correct one, by misguided information or mere chance, we must find a new way to discover the correct direction. So, I am proposing that we focus our efforts first and foremost on the paradigmatic bad ways. In this sense, we can think of the journey as a process of elimination. In other words, get rid of all of the negative space, in hopes that it will provide an ample amount of positive space. Going back to the "Oregon Trail" we should explore some possible routes and see if those are even remotely tenable. Once we find out that a particular path is impossible, we then close off that option. We then repeat this over and over, until we are more limited with our available options. Now I am not proposing that we are in a position that we can always eliminate paths or that we can necessarily narrow down the number of paths. However, I think that this is our best shot. This textbook is about critical thinking and logic, but remember that most of the topics explored here are about poor modes of reasoning. Once you have completed this textbook, you will have a perspicacious understanding of good reasoning.

SECTION II

Basic Concepts/ Terms

a. What is Logic?

1. Logic is a method for structuring language and thoughts. If we go back to the *Organon*, written by Aristotle, we can begin to understand the purpose of logic.[1] He thought that logic was the instrument (Organon) through which we formulate and analyze what science involves. In this sense, logic can be seen as part of metaphysics. We naturally have the desire to know, as he clearly states in his work "Metaphysics."[2] We begin our journey with our senses to provide us with a picture of reality. Aristotle was a philosophical naturalist, which means that he was interested in the physical world. He thought that there was no need to introduce complicated supernatural forces to account for all phenomena. He thought that reality is adequately understood by the laws of nature and human free will. Thus, if we begin our journey to knowledge with experience and sensation, then we must try to explain these experiences to others. Most people are not interested in a merely idiosyncratic view of the world. We want to share our experiences and hence share our understanding of the world. This is evidenced by the fact that in our contemporary world, social media has provided people with the opportunity to share our experience with people who would otherwise never have known. Thus, once we have our rich experiences about the world, we are then inclined to share them with others. Language then becomes the vehicle, so to speak, in which we take the experiential sentiments and verbalize them into a coherent set of symbols to convey to others. I think this, then, becomes the first obstacle for humanity. Mainly, the struggle to put our subjective and personal experiences into concepts and words. Many times we are either unable or unwilling to do so with careful time

[1] Aristotle, Owen F. Octavius, and Porphyry. *The Organon, or Logical Treatises, of Aristotle*. London: G. Bell and Sons, 1883. Print.

[2] Aristotle, and W. D. Ross. *Aristotle's Metaphysics*. Oxford England: Clarendon Press, 1981. Print.

and consideration. Logic is the way in which we put a particular language together. Aristotle and many others have recognized that language has limits and particular ways in which it can function correctly.

Logic, then, has three primary functions for the introductory student. One is the way in which we put our claims together to make sense of our experience. We may readily call this the syntactic function. Syntax has to do with grammar and punctuation. For example, the way in which we structure a sentence. This applies to sentences and arguments as well. Just as improper grammar and punctuation can hamper your ability to understand a sentence, poor syntax may hamper your ability to understand an argument. There are better and worse ways to put together a sentence. The better you are at putting the sentences together, the better that others can clearly understand the meanings of these expressions. This applies to arguments as well. When claims are put together in a definite and concise way that moves organically from one claim to the next, the progression of the argument is explicit. The sentence structure, and also argument structure, can aid one in determining the meaning of the expression.

This brings us to the second function of logic, semantics. If syntax has to do with structure, then semantics has to do with the meanings of the terms, both practically and conceptually. There is an efficient way of using language, such as when I say, "Put the book on the table." In this way, the meanings of the words "book" and "table" have very practical meanings. The collection of papers that are bound together with a title, and the object that is a flat surface in which we can place objects. There is also a conceptual aspect to the meanings of these terms. When I say the word "table," I have a concept in mind. This concept of a table must include a set of conditions that make it that thing apart from other things. We call these essential or necessary conditions. Many people, even those who have not been classically trained in a formal setting, are capable of using language in an efficient way, which serves well for ordinary conversation. However, when we are attempting to be technical and precise, as science often requires, then ordinary usage will not suffice. We will need to delve into the conceptual realm to establish the essential characteristics that make up the thing. Here is where Aristotle thinks that logic comes into play. He wants to make sure that language can adequately describe reality in order to analyze science.[3] He thinks that logic has to do with subjects and predicates. He believes that predicates are real and exist outside of the mind. Thus, the predicates of being tall, articulate, standing, and so on are real predicates that exist independent of the perceiver's mind. So, language is our vehicle to express concepts and referents. These two functions of logic are methodical.

The third primary function of logic is based upon principles. We are quite acclimated to hearing empty platitudes such as: "anything is possible if you focus your mind." or "that there are virtually no limits on the mind, it being infinitely possible." These proverbs are

[3] Aristotle, Own F. Octavius, and Porphyry. *The Organon, or Logical Treatises, of Aristotle*. London: G. Bell and Sons, 1883. Print.

potentially inspiring or uplifting, but they are patently false. The more appropriate proverb should be something along the lines of "if you can conceptualize it, then it is logically possible." This fits better with our understanding of logic. For, if something is not conceptually possible, then it is not logically possible. If I were to ask you to "Conceptualize a round-square or a ball that is simultaneously red and green all over," then I bet you would have a difficult time doing this. Why is that the case, not just for you but all of humanity? You are not able to conceptualize round-squares because this proposition is expressing a contradiction. Contradictions are impossible both physically and conceptually. Thus, the principles of thought present us with concepts that are impossible and concepts that are necessarily true. An example of the latter would be that either an object is red or it is non-red. One of those predicates must necessarily be attached to a subject. For, if it is the case that it is red, then it cannot be the case that it is non-red. Similarly, if it is the case that it is non-red, then it cannot be the case that it is red. Since it cannot both be red and non-red simultaneously, it follows that it is either red or non-red. There are no other options. Red and non-red are jointly sufficient, meaning that together, they encapsulate all the available possibilities, and hence a third option does not exist.

Logic is an organized method and a set of principles that helps us coherently express our experiences, and evaluates arguments. The methodical approach helps us construct, analyze, and scrutinize arguments. The principle-based approach helps us find the limits on the mind and confines us to this logical space.

2. There is a difference between a subjective claim and an objective claim. A subjective claim is such that its truth depends entirely upon the individual. Without the individual, there would be no truth. Subjective claims are peculiar, changing, uncertain, and sometimes emotional. An example of this would be, "Sushi is good." Although many people are inclined to agree with this statement, there are also many others who are not. We are inclined to make a leap from here and say that since we cannot wholeheartedly agree on this, then there is no answer. Keep in mind though, just because we cannot agree on something, does not mean that there is no given truth in the situation. People disagree about whether or not God exists, but the fact that people disagree does not mean that there is no fact of the matter as to whether or not God exists. The claim, "Sushi is good" is a subjective claim because its truth depends on the individual, hence me. If I were not present to make such a claim, then there would be no truth to the proposition. *Goodness* is not an ordinary property found in objects like others. *Goodness* is a term used to regard something, in particular, positively. Thus, it depends on an individual to regard that something. Objective claims do not function in the same way. An objective claim is a fact of the matter that does not depend on an individual to be so. Objective claims are a certain way independent of thoughts, feelings, or emotions. Objective claims are universal, unchanging, absolute, and measurable. For example, an objective claim would be that the earth is round. Although many people believed at one point that it was flat, it was round. The shape of the earth was a certain way independent of what we thought about it. In this sense, objective claims are neutral to human influence.

When providing an argument to others, we are trying to convince them that this position is the best of all options and that it is backed up by facts. Thus, facts need to be objective. Otherwise, we run the risk of "Alternative Facts" that run us around in circles.[4] I imagine that most people can think of a time in which the establishment of an objective fact results in the temporary suspension of the debate. When facts are clear, verifiable and/or measurable, then we have the best chance of drawing inferences. Drawing an inference is also objective. It is a method by which we move logically from one claim to the next. In this way, logic must be objective. For example, suppose I form the belief that it is snowing outside. The fact that I believe it is snowing has no impact on the truth of the matter. Either it is snowing outside, or it is not. My belief does not have the meteorological power to control the weather. I may believe that it is snowing outside when it is actually snowing outside. The evidence for this does not depend on me believing it. We have clear and measurable evidence that it is snowing. Arguments need to function similarly. Your subjective experiences are not well suited to prove objective conclusions about the world. So, subjective claims are not able to prove objective claims. Thus, the starting point for logic is, to begin with, objectivity.

Objectivity and rationality are distinct yet similar concepts. Being rational is to form a belief system that conforms to reason. When we act, we have adopted a set of reasons. I might have an inkling for sushi, and then after work, I go to a sushi restaurant. In that way, my reason for acting is a direct result of my belief that sushi is good, the hunger that I feel at a point in time, and my ability to merge those two beliefs. So, in order to be a "rational animal," as Aristotle refers to humans, we must make sure that our beliefs about the world align with the facts in an honest, consistent, and objective way.[5] Some reasons are better than others. This is true of basic actions that you perform on a daily basis, and true for more complex inference drawing.

The following section begins with some basic concepts in logic. We will begin our journey through this text, by starting with argument recognition. The first thing that we need to do is to establish an argument apart from a non-argument.

---

[4] Conway, Kellyanne. Meet the Press interview. 22 Jan. 2017.

[5] Aristotle, W. D. Ross, and Lesley Brown. *The Nicomachean Ethics*. Oxford: Oxford University Press, 2009. Print.

Exercise 2.1

2.1.1 *Directions:* Indicate whether the following statements are true or false:

1. Logic is merely a matter of opinion.
2. Arguments need to be evaluated objectively to determine their internal structure.
3. Ordinary language and argumentative language are essentially the same.
4. All arguments are created equal.
5. You cannot dismiss an argument because you do not like the conclusion.
6. Logic is a set of rules or principles that helps us evaluate arguments.
7. Thinking is a natural mental activity, and we all do it well.
8. Logic discovers relations in our ordinary language.
9. If a set of arguments keeps going in a circle, then that means there is no correct answer.
10. Logic is a skill that needs constant improvement.

2.1.2 *Directions:* Please provide a brief definition for the following terms:

Logic	Syntax	Semantics	Principle	*Objective	Subjective
Rationality	Contradiction	Inference	Fact	Opinion	Truth

b. Arguments

1. The word "argument" has more than one sense. In the ordinary sense, an argument is a verbal fight that you have with another person that involves screaming at each other until someone has had enough. Although there have been certain philosophers that have engaged in such activities, that is not the proper understanding of an argument. Arguments, in the strict logical sense, are a group of statements in which one or more of them is meant to provide evidence for a further statement. In laymen's terms, an argument is a set of claims that leads us naturally to another claim. As I have already stated, not all arguments are created equal. Some of the statements will lead us to the further claim and others will not. However, every group of statements called an "argument" is purporting to provide evidence for a further statement.

   There is a fundamental difference between an apparent proof and an actual proof. An apparent proof has all of the basic symptoms of an argument, but they lack the property of entailment. In other words, the claims do not function together properly to lead us to that further statement. An actual proof has all of the symptoms of an argument including the entailment of the further statement. This is why many arguments have a surface plausibility to the non-refined thinker. Hence, without proper training, you will be more inclined to accept an apparent proof instead of the adequately structured actual proof.

   Arguments are entirely different from expressing subjective opinions about a particular subject. If I say, "Sushi is good," then I am merely expressing a subjective view that I have about sushi, but not that all people should say the same. It is equally possible that two people could hold the complete opposite view about sushi. I am not contesting such a claim. On the other hand, when I say, "Murder is bad" I am not expressing the same sentiment as the former. The claim that "Murder is bad" is meant to be a universal proposition that regards murder as being a grotesque act not only for me but also for any member of the human race. If the claim, "Murder is bad" is identical to saying "Sushi is good," then we would have to allow that two people can hold opposite views with the same amount of truth. When I say, "Murder is bad," I am saying that murder is wrong and ought to be forbidden for me and all others. I am attempting to deny the opposite position with an argument. We do not expect the same thing as the other example. When someone says, "Sushi is good," neither do I demand an argument nor do I attempt to refute such a claim. However, in the case of murder, that is what we are attempting to do.

   This shows us the first component of an argument; mainly it is attempting to prove the further claim, that is, the hypothesis. We can think of the word "hypothesis" to mean a claim that is not self-evident, it is debatable, and is in need of further evidence.

   A statement is a declarative sentence. Declarative sentences do precisely what the name states, that is, it declares something to either be the case or not be the case. In this introductory text, we will restrict declarative sentences to a relation between a subject and a predicate.

So, a declarative sentence is declaring that a particular subject either has or lacks a specific predicate at a point in time. Declarative sentences are either true or false. The easiest test to see whether a sentence is declarative or not is to preface the sentence with the following:

It is true or false that ___*insert sentence*___.

If you insert the sentence to this formula and the sentence no longer makes sense, then it is not a statement. If you insert the sentence to this formula and the sentence does make sense, then it is a statement. Some sentences are not statements. For example, questions and exclamations are not statements, even though they are sentences. All statements are sentences, but it does not follow that all sentences are statements. Elementary logic uses binary logic. Thus, we will use bivalent logic, that is, classical logic that deals with truth and falsity. Logic is not confined to bivalency exclusively. There are three-valued logical systems, many-valued logical systems, degree theory, and fuzzy logic. Although these are worthy of study, this text is focused on bivalent logic.

Truth and falsity are called truth-values. A truth-value is the assignment of truth or falsity to a particular statement. A statement is said to be true, if and only if, there is a state of affairs that corresponds to the linguistic vehicle of the expression. For example, if I were to say, "The marker is blue," then that statement is true, if and only if, there is a state of affairs such that there is a subject referred to as a marker, and that *marker* is exemplifying the property of *blueness*. If the state of affairs were such that the marker is *red*, then the statement "The marker is blue" is false. Statements need to correspond to facts about the world in order to be classified as true, and anything otherwise is false. Every statement is either true or false, and this is called the principle of bivalence. To be clear, even though every statement is true or false, does not mean that we know or will ever know that truth. There might be statements that are epistemically closed off to us. This does not mean that there is no truth, but that we do not know the truth.

When looking at an argument, you should be able to distinguish the support claims from the hypothesis. The support claims are needed to provide evidence for the hypothesis, without which the hypothesis is not proven. An argument includes one or more support claims and only one conclusion. This will help when trying to find the hypothesis. Suppose you encounter an argument that has more than one conclusion. This means one of two things. First, the person arguing is incompetent, and they are using multiple conclusion indicator words, when in fact, they should be using other indicator words. Second, is that the passage contains more than one argument. When a passage contains more than one argument, it can be quite difficult to establish which support claims go with which hypotheses. The best way to find the support claims and the claim that is supported, is to look for certain indicator words. These indicator words tell you if the statement is a support claim or the claim being supported. The evidence claims are called premises. The term "premise" means that it is a support claim or evidence for the hypothesis. The claim that is in need of support is called the "conclusion".[6] Remember that an argument contains only *one* conclusion but one or more premises.

[6] I have been referring to it as the hypothesis. Henceforth, you may use the word "conclusion" or "hypothesis" synonymously to refer to the claim that is in need of support.

Here are some premise indicator words:

since because for as given that the fact that it follows from
as indicated by for the reason that assuming that as shown by
may be inferred from

Here are some conclusion indicator words:

therefore wherefore thus it follows that conclusively accordingly
so we may conclude we may infer consequently hence
which implies that in conclusion

As an introductory student to logic, these lists can be confusing at the very least. Many students will confuse the two sets and think that a premise indicator is a conclusion indicator and vice versa. Thus, I would like to propose a more straightforward way of familiarizing yourself with these terms. Since an argument only contains one conclusion and one or more premises, the best method is to use the process of elimination. Instead of focusing on the premise indicator words, spend some time learning all of the conclusion indicator words. Then, when you encounter a passage, and you are trying to find the conclusion and the premises, look for the conclusion indicator word. Once you find the conclusion indicator word, you know that the statement that follows is the conclusion. That means that all of the other statements are premises. Once you are familiar with the conclusion indicator list and you have a better understanding of argument structure, then you can go back and learn all of the premise indicator words.

Once the premises and the conclusion have been established, then you need to write the argument out in the standard form. This includes listing the premises first with the most important at the top and the conclusion at the bottom. Look at the following examples:

(1) All men are mortal.
(2) Socrates is a man.
Therefore, Socrates is a mortal.

(1) All men are mortal.
(2) Socrates is a mortal.
Therefore, Socrates is a man.

Both of the arguments above are in standard form. The most important premise (major premise) is listed first, the next premise (minor premise) is listed second, and the conclusion is listed last.[7]

[7] The major premise and minor premise are concepts that are introduced here, but are not explained until section 5 of this text. For brevity's sake, a thorough explanation is not essential at this point.

If you evaluate the two arguments listed above, you will notice that they are not of the same form. They appear to be very similar to one another. In fact, many people reason in this kind of way. They think that both arguments are drawing appropriate inferences. The argument on the left is one in which the premises do support the conclusion, whereas the argument on the right is one in which the premises do not support the conclusion, even though it purports to do so.

An inference is the reasoning process that is contained in an argument. In other words, it is the process by which we move from a set of statements to a further statement that is supported by the former statements. The goal in logic, then, is to learn the best methods for drawing inferences and being able to determine when a poor inference has been drawn.

2. An inference is a process of moving from a set of statements to a further claim. I have already stated that some statements lead naturally to a further claim and others that do not. We classify the former as arguments that possess an inferential connection. Think of the inferential connection as a function of the constituent parts. When the parts (statements) of an argument are put together in such a way that we are led to further statements, the argument is said to have an inferential connection. If the passage is lacking that function, then the argument does not have an inferential connection nor does it prove anything. A passage that lacks the inferential connection is not an argument, in any sense, and is a group of random statements with no relation to one another. Have a look at the following example:

   Some professors are grouchy.
   Cats are creepy.
   Therefore, all dogs go to heaven.

   These statements have nothing to do with one another. It might be the case that the premises and the conclusion are true, but the truth of these statements do not possess the inferential connection. Consider the following argument:

   All glorps are gleeps.
   All gleeps are glocks.
   Therefore, all glorps are glocks.

   These statements are not true because there are no states of affairs to prove that the subjects and predicates relate to one another. However, you should recognize that these statements do possess the inferential connection. If every member belonging to the "glorp" class is included in the set of the "gleep" class, and every member of the "gleep" class is included in the "glock" class, then it follows with certainty that all members of the "glorp" class are included in the "glock" class. Truth and the inferential connection are different concepts.

An inferential connection can be either explicit or implicit. "Explicit" in this context, is clearly and overtly stated as such. "Implicit" is not clearly and overtly stated, but implied. If the inferential connection is explicit, then the passage will contain specific terminology that signifies there is a connection. Note the following example: Since all men are mortal, and Socrates is a man, it follows with certainty that Socrates is a mortal.

The explicit use of the words "since," "and," and "it follows with certainty" show you that this passage contains an argument. The word "since" is a premise indicator; the word "and" is a conjunction that is joining the two premises together, and lastly the phrase "it follows with certainty" is a conclusion indicator that is stating which statement follows from the other two. Explicit indicator words help us determine the inferential connection. Thus, indicator words provide you with an explicit inferential connection. An inferential connection does not need to be explicitly stated with indicator words. Consider the following example:

> The a/c unit in my car is in need of repair. I filled the a/c unit with a can of Freon R-134a. I checked to make sure that the pulley was working correctly, and it was freely moving without any sticking. I replaced the belt to see if that resolved anything, and none of those things worked.

This passage contains an inferential connection, and thus it is an argument. The inferential connection is not explicit, but it is implicit. The hypothesis is "The a/c unit in my car is in need of repair" and is in need of support. If you were to take your car into the dealership and tell them this, they would ask you for reasons. It would be absurd for them to repair the a/c unit because you said so. From the facts that I filled the a/c unit with the liquid that cools the air, checked the system that operates the a/c unit, and made a minor repair to the main part that does run the a/c unit provides you with a strong indication that there is a problem with the a/c unit itself. When an argument has an implicit inferential connection, the conclusion is stated first. The reason for this is that the bold hypothesis is stated first, and then the support claims follow from that. If the conclusion was listed halfway through the passage, then this would confuse the reader/listener to a point in which they would not be able to reason through the argument. That is not to say that a conclusion never appears in the middle of an argument. This happens quite frequently. The only difference is that when the conclusion is posited halfway through the argument, the inferential connection is usually explicit. Again, there might be an occasion when the inferential connection is not explicit, and the conclusion is listed halfway through the argument. In this text, however, all examples that use an implicit inferential connection will list the conclusion first. Upon completion of this text, you will possess the ability to find the conclusion no matter where it is located in the argument.

Exercise 2.2

2.2.1 *Directions:* Indicate whether the following statements are true or false:

1. A premise is set forth as evidence for the conclusion.
2. A conclusion does not need any evidence for it to be true.
3. All arguments must contain a conclusion indicator word.
4. A proposition is a declarative sentence that is either true or false.
5. "Since," "therefore," "so," and "consequently" are all conclusion indicator words.
6. An implicit claim is one in which it is clearly and overtly stated.
7. An explicit claim alludes to specific meaning but does not overtly state it.
8. An inference is the reasoning process expressed by an argument.
9. An argument is unique in the sense that it is trying to *prove* something to be the case.
10. All sentences are statements.

2.2.2 *Directions:* Provide a brief definition of the following terms:

Premise	Conclusion	Argument
Inferential Connection	Proposition	Inference
Conclusion Indicator	Premise Indicator	Explicit
Implicit	Truth-value	Objectivity

2.2.3 *Direction:* All of the following are arguments. Determine the premises and conclusion of each argument. List the premises first, and the conclusion last.

1. Elementary logic, in the technical sense of the term, is that part of the symbolic or mathematical logic in which the notions of "all" and "some" are applied only to individuals and not also to classes or attributes or individuals. It is at once the most substantial part of the subject and the most straightforward part that permits a wide variety of non-trivial applications. Consequently, it seems especially suitable for study by beginners.[8]

2. It seems that God does not exist; because if one of two contraries be infinite, the other would be altogether destroyed. But, the name God means that He is infinite goodness. If, therefore, God existed, there would be no evil discoverable; but there is evil in the world. Therefore God does not exist.[9]

[8] Mates, Benson. *Elementary Logic*. Symbolic Logic 38 Oxford: Oxford University Press, 1973. Print.

[9] Aquinas, Thomas. *The Summa Theologica of St. Thomas Aquinas*. London: Burns Oates & Washbourne, 1912. Print. Aquinas presents this atheistic argument against the existence of God in *Summa Theologica Article Three: Whether God Exists?*, even though he does not endorse this view. After constructing an argument against the existence of God, he then proceeds to prove the existence of God in five different ways.

3. A good flute-player, sculptor, artist, carpenter, etc., is a person who performs his function well. By analogy, if man has a function, a good man will be one who performs his function well. If there is some activity that is peculiar to man, that will be his function. Rational activity is peculiar to man. Therefore, rational activity is man's function.[10]

*4. The Saiga antelope is an animal. Because the Saiga antelope is a mammal, and all mammals are animals.

5. The United States has one of the highest corporate tax rates in the world. The globalization of the world economy has made markets extremely competitive. The only way to incentivize domestic economic growth is to be competitive in the global economy. It follows that the United States needs to lower the corporate tax rate below the current 35% margin.

6. Vaccinations have eradicated many life-threatening diseases over the past one-hundred years or so. The Pulse Polio vaccination alone has helped drop the number of reported cases in India from 28,757 to 3,265 over the span of ten years. In March of 2014, the World Health Organization declared India a polio-free country. Hence, vaccinations are essential to the well-being of the population.[11]

7. If people desire something, then that thing is desirable. Each person desires his own happiness. Thus, each person's happiness is desirable to that person.[12]

8. The world has many objective features independent of my mind. However, I am confined to viewing the world through the lenses of my mind. If I am only able to see the world through my mental lenses, then I do not know the objective features of the world. So, I do not have access to the objective features of the world.[13]

9. Either this class will be exhilarating, or this class will be a nightmare. Considering the amount of tedious and rigorous work that this class requires, it is undoubtedly not exhilarating. It must be the case that this class is a nightmare.

10. Things are either the case or not the case. For, if something is the case, then it is impossible not to be the case. Similarly, if something is not the case, it is impossible for it to be the case. Accordingly, a thing cannot be the case and not be the case simultaneously without implying a contradiction.

---

[10] Aristotle, W. D. Ross, and Lesley Brown. *The Nicomachean Ethics*. Oxford: Oxford University Press, 2009. Print.

[11] World Health Organization. http://www.searo.who.int/immunization/topics/polio/eradication/sea-polio-free/en/. 2018. Website.

[12] Mill, John Stuart. *The Basic Writings of John Stuart Mill: On Liberty, the Subjection of Women, and Utilitarianism*. New York: Modern Library, 2002. Print.

[13] Kant, Immanuel and Norman K. Smith. *Immanuel Kant's Critique of Pure Reason*. Boston: Bedford, 1929. Print.

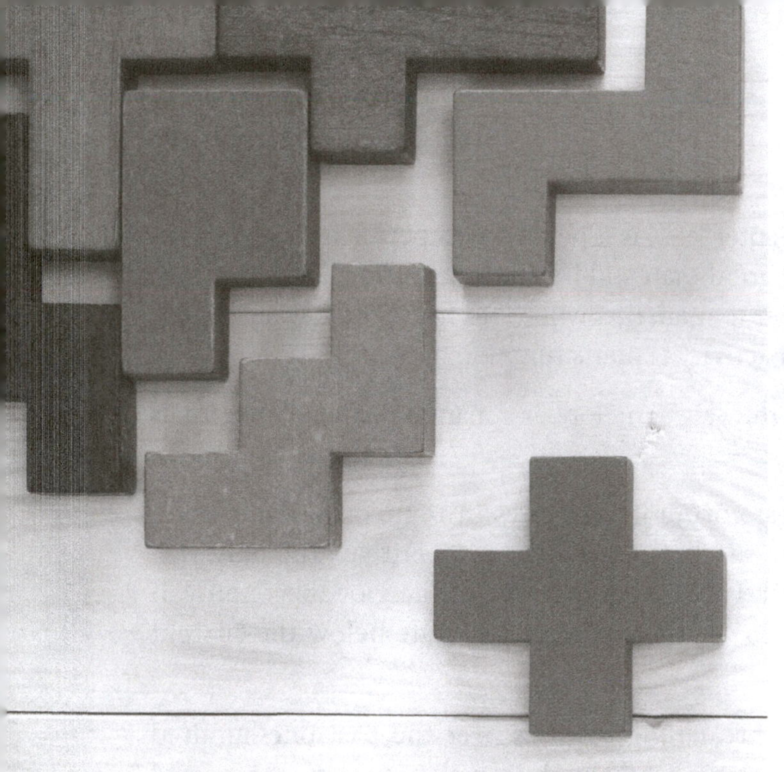

SECTION III

Argument Recognition

a. Support claims and claims in need of support

1. As discussed in the previous section, some claims support further claims, and some claims are in need of support. The method that was introduced to see whether a sentence is a declarative sentence or not is a quick and easy process. Thus, a very similar method can be used to check and see if the claim is intended for support or is in need of support. The word "because" is a premise indicator. It signifies to the reader/listener that the claim which follows it is a premise supporting a further claim. When an arguer asserts a bold hypothesis, it would seem strange to use the word "because" before it. Especially, when you keep in mind that a hypothesis is a debatable claim that needs to be proven. To use the word "because" before a claim that is not well accepted seems to be mistaken. To remedy this, the words "because" and "therefore" should be used to test whether the statement is a premise or a conclusion. If you place the word "because" before a statement and no longer makes sense, then that means that the statement is more than likely a conclusion. Conversely, if you place the word "therefore" before a statement and it makes no sense either, then the statement is more than likely a premise.

   When evaluating a passage to determine whether it is an argument or a non-argument, you should keep a few things in mind. The following method is a checklist to help you determine if a passage contains an argument. The first thing to check is whether the central claim is in need of proof. That is, does the bold hypothesis need to be proven or is that already accepted? It should become evident that "already accepted" is somewhat vague. In this context, an acceptable hypothesis is one in which a competent person with a primary K-12 education would readily agree. "Competency," here means that the person has completed all required training in K-12 while earning the bare minimum GPA of 2.0 or above.

The second thing that you need to look out for is the inferential connection (either explicitly or implicitly). You will find the inferential connection by looking for certain indicator words listed in the previous section. More importantly, it requires that you evaluate the passage and see if there is any connection between the statements that lead us to further claims. You can always use the "because/therefore" test to see if the statements are proving some further statement or are in need of proof.

b. No inferential connection

1. Beliefs are a fundamental part of being a human being. It is essential that you have beliefs about the world that shape you as a human being. Thus, it is quite simply the acceptance of a claim. When you believe a particular proposition, then you have internally accepted that claim. Now just because you have accepted the claim, does not necessarily mean that the proposition is true. We certainly hope that our beliefs are true. However, it is possible that we hold beliefs that we think are true, but are, in fact, false. Once we recognize this, we will readily see that a belief is conceptually different from the truth. Statements and/or arguments are not true merely because the person believes them to be the case. The fact that you believe a claim has no impact on the truth or falsity of such claims. Although it is important that you form beliefs about the world, these beliefs themselves are not proper evidence for the hypothesis. As we have discussed in the last section, arguments need objectivity, mainly facts that are independent of the particular circumstances of the individual. So, when a person says that they believe x; therefore, x must be true, they are not being objective in their pursuits. Since the belief itself is only the acceptance of a claim, it is not considered evidence.

   For example, many people believed that the earth was flat. This consensus among thinkers had no impact on the truth or falsity of such claims. It seems as though the truth of the proposition, "The earth is round" has nothing to do with whether or not people believed it to be the case.

2. Reports are not as commonly thought of as arguments. Reports are not a fundamental part of being a human being. Reports are a way in which we convey information about some particular event or phenomena. Reports are strictly conveying facts that have already occurred. In this sense, reports are not arguments. Arguments are meant to prove that something is the case and not merely stating what has happened. Reports do not include any inferential connection whatsoever. Reports are commonly used during news broadcasts. In this way, they are conveying information to viewers about what has already occurred. It is quite rare for a news broadcast to prove that something is the case. However, it is worth noting that there are investigatory journalists who do uncover stories and prove hypotheses. These are not usually done on local and evening news sources. Thus, a report will present a list of facts that are objectively

measured, but it does not attempt to prove that something is the case, it merely presented what has already occurred.

3. An explanation is different from an argument because the former is merely stating why something is the case, but not trying to prove that it is the case. An explanation includes a claim that is already well accepted by the listeners, and thus it shows how and/or why that came into being. In this sense, explanations reason backward from the effect to the cause. Arguments reason from the cause to the effect. Arguments are meant to prove something that is not already accepted. We have already accepted that the effect has come into being. Once we have already established that truth, then there is no need to prove that hypothesis. An explanation is used when we are to consider why that effect was brought about. One should be careful though, for most explanations use the word "because" which is a premise indicator. Keep in mind that the use of the word "because" does not necessarily mean that the passage is an argument. When an explanation uses the word "because," it is being used in a temporal sense. It is referring to the order in time in which the effect came into being.

   For example, the flag appears red from my perspective because there are wavelengths at 680 nanometers of light refraction bouncing off the object. This is not proving that the flag appears red. For neuroscientists have proven that colors are not in the world. When I say that the flag appears red, I am not saying anything contentious that is in need of proof. For anyone who has either seen the flag or can imagine seeing a red flag has already accepted that claim. So, there is no proof here. I am merely explaining why the flag appears red and not proving that it appears red.

   Some explanations can also be classified as an argument as well. In this sense, sometimes explanations contain an inferential connection, which all depends on the hypothesis. If the hypothesis is not already accepted or is not considered a fact, then it is probably an argument. This relies entirely on the audience. For if I were to present the former example about wavelengths of light refraction to a society that is not well versed in neuroscience, then that particular society may be inclined to call this passage an argument. However, since we are well versed in the advancements of neuroscience, this passage is a mere explanation.

4. Conditional statements are one of the most fundamental components of logic. In fact, conditional statements will be used throughout this entire book. A conditional statement is best characterized as an "if, then" statement.

   If you are a lawyer, then you went to law school.
   If you are a conservative, then you believe in traditional values.

   The conditional statement has two component parts. First, is the *antecedent*, and follows the word "if." The second is the *consequent*, and follows the word "then." Sometimes the statement is not in the standard "if, then" form. You will occasionally see something as follows:

   Healthcare premiums will rise if the Affordable Care Act is passed.

This is not the standard conditional statement form, but it is still conditional. Remember, the term that follows the word "if" is the antecedent. So, in this example, "the Affordable Care Act is passed" is the antecedent and "Healthcare premiums will rise" is the consequent. You will readily see that conditionals take on two forms with the standard one listed first.

If *antecedent*, then *consequent.*

Consequent, if *antecedent.*

A conditional statement is a hypothetical statement. Hypothetical statements do not express an actual truth, but merely a hypothetical one. That is, they express the idea that if the antecedent is satisfied, then so too is the consequent. It is equally possible for the antecedent to be false, and the consequent to be true or false; the antecedent true, and the consequent true; thus, the only time a conditional is false is when the antecedent is true, and the consequent is false. The reason for this will be adequately explained in the later sections, but a brief explanation is in order. Conditional statements are trying to show that if the antecedent is the case, then the consequent must follow. In this way, the consequent depends on the antecedent to be the case. For if the antecedent is the case, but it is possible that consequent does not follow, then the conditional is not adequately understood as such.

A conditional statement is not an argument. An argument is a group of statements, one or more of which is intended to prove or provide evidence for another claim. A conditional statement is only a statement and not a group of statements. One conditional statement cannot be an argument any more than one individual statement can be an argument. If so, then the conditional statement would be the premise and the conclusion, which is *begging the question* (a fallacy covered later in this book). However, just because a conditional statement cannot be an argument by itself, does not mean that it cannot be part of an argument. Arguments may include conditionals as a part. Mainly, it could be one or more premises and/or the conclusion. Note the following examples:

If it is a cat, then it is an animal.

It is a cat.

Therefore, it is an animal.

If it is an A, then it is a B.

If it is a B, then it is a C.

Therefore, if it is an A, then it is a C.

Conditional statements are centrally crucial in logic because they express the relation between a sufficient and a necessary condition. First of all, we need to establish the difference between the two. A necessary condition is one that is needed to get the job done such that if the necessary condition is not satisfied, then the job will not get done. Think of the necessary condition as an essential part of the task at hand. A sufficient condition is enough to the get the job done. However, it is worth noting that just because a sufficient condition gets the job done, does not mean that it is also necessary. There may be other ways in which you could get the job done. In this way, sufficient is an optional condition among many that are capable of completing the task at hand. The easiest way to see this is by example.

Consider the word "bachelor" and think about what is needed to be classified as such. It is possible to consider a handful of things that are contingently found amongst bachelors but are not central to *being* a bachelor. Many people think that this includes but is not limited to: being rich, good-looking, having your own place, a stable job, and the like. These are only accidental conditions of bachelorhood. It is possible to imagine a person whom is labeled a bachelor and is lacking all of these contingencies. However, in order to be a bachelor, there must be a set of characteristics (necessary conditions) that make the person a bachelor (sufficient condition) and not a non-bachelor. In order to be classified as a bachelor appropriately one must be a man and unmarried. If the person in question is married, then they are not a bachelor. If the person in question is not a man, then they are not a bachelor. In this sense, these are not accidental or contingent features, but necessary features of being a bachelor. Many people think that is all that is needed to be a bachelor. Although those two features might suffice, I think that we can refine this concept a bit more. I think that age is a requirement for bachelorhood. I am not in any position to classify what that age must be. At certain times throughout history, the age has been extraordinarily young—eleven years of age, and at other times it has been much higher—eighteen years of age. The important matter here is that age must be considered regarding the time in which it is not only accepted but possible to marry. I take this to be a fundamental component of bachelorhood. One thing is clear to me that a newborn baby is not a bachelor. If we go back to one of the first necessary conditions, mainly being a man, then we should see that a newborn baby is not yet a man. Although the newborn baby has the potential to be a man, they are not yet a man any more than an acorn is an oak tree. It would be grossly inappropriate and conceptually flawed to classify a newborn baby as a bachelor. When I say that age is a necessary condition of being a bachelor, I mean that coming of age to be a man is central to being a bachelor. I can also think of one person in particular whom is not considered a bachelor and yet has satisfied all three of the necessary conditions. The Pope is not a bachelor even though he is a man, unmarried, and of age. He is not a bachelor because he is not eligible to marry. The Pope is married to God and the Church and took a vow of celibacy. Thus, because the Pope is not eligible to marry, he is not a bachelor. I think that the list of man, unmarried, age, and eligible is enough to get the point across. Each of these is a necessary condition, and collectively they are sufficient to classify a person as a bachelor.

You might be wondering about other cases of *bachelorhood*. For one, how about people who are divorced? If you get a divorce, do you go back to being a bachelor? Alternatively, do we think of being a bachelor as a once a lifetime type of thing such that once you lose it, then it has gone forever? What about a person who is a widow? Are they returning to being a bachelor or not? These bring up some fascinating cases in which to consider. These topics are beyond the scope of this course, and for brevity's sake, we will leave those for another time.

Conditional statements express the relation between a sufficient and a necessary condition. So, I want you to imagine two cases; the first is when you have a necessary condition and try to derive the sufficient condition; secondly when you have a sufficient condition and try to derive the necessary condition. You should immediately recognize that you cannot go from a necessary condition to the sufficient condition without assuming many other necessary conditions.

On the other hand, it is easy to see how you can go from a sufficient condition to one of the necessary conditions. Remember that the sufficient condition encapsulates all of the necessary conditions such that if you provide the sufficient condition, you are implicitly providing all of the necessary conditions. So, when I provide the sufficient condition, I can provide the necessary condition as well. The converse is not true. If the sufficient condition includes many necessary conditions, then you are not able to move from the single necessary condition to the sufficient (many necessary conditions) condition. For example, "If you are a man, then you are a bachelor" is not true. Just because you have satisfied one of the necessary conditions does not mean that you are sufficiently a bachelor. The converse of this will work though "If you are a bachelor, then you are a man." You should be able to surmise the relation of sufficient and necessary conditions that apply to conditional statements. "If *sufficient*, then *necessary*" but not "If *necessary*, then *sufficient*."

Exercise 3.1

3.1.1 *Directions:* Indicate whether the following statements are true or false:

1. Reports are meant to convey information and prove a hypothesis.
2. An explanation reasons backward whereas an argument reasons forward.
3. Believing a claim guarantees that the claim is true.
4. A conditional statement always begins with the antecedent.
5. Some explanations are considered arguments as well.
6. If you have a sufficient condition, then you can derive a necessary condition.
7. If you have a necessary condition, then you can derive a sufficient condition.
8. In order to distinguish an argument from a non-argument, you must consider the audience that is being presented with the material.
9. A conditional statement includes an antecedent and a conclusion.
10. Conclusions occasionally need to be proven.

3.1.2 *Directions:* Insert the word "sufficient" or "necessary" to make the following statements true:

1. Being a man is a ________________ condition for being a bachelor.

*2. Being a bachelor is a ________________ condition for being unmarried.

3. Being a professor is a ________________ condition for being a person with a graduate degree.
4. Being a person with a graduate degree is a ________________ condition for being a professor.
5. Having a set of golf clubs is a ________________ condition for playing golf.
6. Having granulated sugar is a ________________ condition for making sugar cookies.
7. A belief is a ______________ condition for knowledge.
8. Being a polygon is a ________________ condition for being a triangle.
9. Being a square is a ________________ condition for being a polygon.
10. Being engaged in the material is a ________________ condition for understanding a lecture.

3.1.3 *Directions:* Determine whether the following passages contain an argument or a non-argument. If it contains an argument, then provide the conclusion. If it contains a non-argument, then write either "report," "belief," "explanation," or "conditional statement."

1. The assassination of Archduke Franz Ferdinand of Austria occurred on June 28, 1914. This assassination was meant to merge the southern provinces of Austria-Hungary with Yugoslavia. Austria-Hungary then declared war, which began World War 1 including most of the European nations.
2. Wine no longer makes my heart glad; a little of it makes me sad, much makes me melancholy. My soul is faint and impotent; in vain I prick the spur of pleasure into its flank, its strength is gone, it rises no more to the royal leap. I have lost my illusions. Vainly I seek to plunge myself into the boundless sea of joy; it cannot sustain me, or rather, I cannot sustain myself.[1]
3. If John is a kleptomaniac, then John enjoys stealing incessantly. If John steals incessantly, then John is untrustworthy. Thus, if John is a kleptomaniac, then John is untrustworthy.
4. Golden retrievers are great dogs for people with children. They are trained to retrieve animals while hunting. They are gentle enough not to kill or damage the animal that they are retrieving. They have a very soft bite such that they can hold an egg in their jaw without breaking it. Because of this, it is quite safe to have children around a golden retriever without a fear of the dog biting and harming the child.
5. The catfish is called that name because of the barbel whiskers that resemble that of a cat.
6. If we increase restrictions on whom can purchase a weapon and the duration of the background check, then we will have fewer gun violence in this country.
7. Things are in motion. Those things in motion were put into motion by another. For nothing can put itself in motion. Only that which is in actual motion can push something in potential motion into actual motion. Thus, since all things in motion are in motion because of another thing in motion, this either goes back to infinity, or there is a purely actualized thing in motion that was always in motion.[2]
8. If the last example was clearly understood, then you understand backward causation. If the last example was not clearly understood, then you do not understand backward causation. Thus, if you did not complete the last example, then you do not understand this example.
9. Pierre Beaumarchais wrote La Folle Journee (The Marriage of Figaro) in 1778. This comedic play was made into an opera in 1786. It follows the day in which the marriage between Suzanne, the Countess' maid; and Figaro, the Count's valet, occurs. Mozart used this play as a catalyst to denounce the aristocratic privilege as a foreshadowing of the French Revolution. Napoleon Bonaparte called it "The Revolution already put into action."[3]

*10. If Duchamp's "The Fountain" is considered art, then anything without exception is considered art.

---

[1] Kierkegaard, Søren, David F. Swenson, Lillian M. Swenson, and Walter Lowrie. *Either/or: A Fragment of Life*. Princeton, N.J.: Princeton University Press, 1946. Print.

[2] Aquinas, Thomas. *The Summa Theologica of St. Thomas Aquinas*. London: Burns Oates & Washbourne, 1912. Print.

[3] Stewart, Austin. *OperaHERE: The Marriage of Figaro*. Macomb Community College (Macomb Multicultural International Initiative Speaker Series), 2017.

c. Induction versus Deduction

1. At this point, we have acquired the tools that are necessary to distinguish between an argument and a non-argument. However, not all arguments are created equal. Some arguments will lead us to the conclusion with necessity; and other arguments will lead us to the conclusion with mere probability; both of which are intended to support their conclusion. An argument is said to be deductive, if and only if, the conclusion follows from the premises with strict necessity. An argument is said to be inductive, if and only if, the conclusion follows from the premises with degrees of probability. In other words, there is a likelihood that the conclusion follows the premises but not a guarantee.

   The following examples illuminate this distinction:

   All books have at least one author.

   The "Organon" is a book.

   Therefore, the "Organon" has at least one author.

   Most books are written by one author.

   The Bible is a book.

   Therefore, the Bible was written by one author.

   The crucial difference between the two of these is the likelihood in which the conclusion follows from the premises. The first example is a deductive argument. The two premises guarantee that the conclusion follows with necessity. In other words, there is no interpretation in which the conclusion does not follow from those premises. The second example is slightly different. Even if one author writes most books, there are many books written by more than one author. So, you cannot infer that because one author writes most books and that you have a book, that it follows with certainty that the book only has one author. In other words, there is an interpretation such that most books are written by one author, and you have a book written by more than one author. So, in this argument, it is only a likelihood that the conclusion follows from the premises.

   This distinction is a somewhat technical one. Distinguishing between an argument and non-argument is rudimentary, and many introductory students have no problem. On the other hand, the difference between inductive and deductive arguments requires time, skill, patience, and practice. There are a few things to keep in mind while evaluating an argument to determine if it is inductive or deductive. The first thing to watch out for is unique indicator words. Apart from ordinary indicator words, unique indicator words reinforce the conclusion and the degree to which it follows from the premises. For example, "probable," "improbable," "likely," "unlikely," "might," and "might not" are unique indicator words that the arguments are inductive. On the other hand, words like "certainly," "necessarily," "without a doubt" are unique indicator words that the arguments are deductive.

The second thing to look out for is the strength of the inferential connection. Deductive arguments have a robust inferential connection such that the conclusion is already contained in the truth of the premises. An inductive argument has an inferential connection as well; however, the conclusion is beyond the immediate truth of the premises. An easy way to differentiate between an inductive argument and a deductive argument is to imagine two concepts with which we are familiar. The first is a paycheck deduction, and the second is inducing a person into a coma. The former is taking away from what we already have. Your gross income is the collection of money that you have earned before taxes over some period of time. Then, the federal and state government pulls money from your gross income to cover your taxes, and thus you are left with your net income. The taxes have been deduced from you gross, i.e., the taxes are taken from what you already have. The latter example of inducing some person into a coma is not the same. Before the person has been induced, they are not yet in a coma. However, the current status of the patient is in support of putting them into a coma. In this sense, we are moving beyond their current state and into another state. When we induce a person into a coma, we are doing so in hopes that it will allow the brain swelling to go down without much damage to the brain cells. Keep in mind, that when we put a person into a coma, it is only likely that this will help. It is not guaranteed that this will help the patient. So, we can conclude that inducing a person into a coma will help the patient with degrees of probability, whereas deducing a 27% federal tax on your gross income will necessarily lead to a significantly less, but exact net income.

The third tool used to distinguish between an inductive argument and a deductive argument is the form of the argument. Much like golf, logic utilizes proper form. Most professional golfers have a similar form to their swing. Thus, by following the strict rules of golf swings and biomechanics, golfers will likely see a maximized swing that allows the ball to travel farther. Although there are the occasional golfers who can deviate from the technical aspects of a proper swing (Happy Gilmore) and do well, it is much less frequent. The deductive forms have the most rigid form and structure, similar to the professional golfers. The inductive forms have a loose and fluid structure that allows for more obscure golf swings, so to speak.

d. Inductive forms

1. Generalizations are inductive arguments in which a small sample is collected and then a claim is made about the entire group. These arguments are helpful if the sample size is representative of the entire group. If the sample is relatively small and obscure, then it is not a useful generalization.

   My Ethics course last semester of about 30 students had ten nursing students.

   Therefore, 1/3 of the students in my Ethics courses are nursing students.

This argument follows with degrees of probability (statistics) in which it is likely from the sample size. It is indeed possible that I teach an Ethics course with more or less than 1/3 being nursing students, however, it is reasonable to assume that nursing students are required to take Ethics more than other disciplines, and thus the courses will consist of those students.

2. An argument based upon authority is one in which the conclusion depends on a claim made by an expert in a particular field.

    The CFO for a Fortune 500 company, said that the quarterly profit earnings are up.

    Therefore, we must conclude that this is indeed true.

    There is no denying the fact that the CFO could be wrong, mistaken, or lied about this. All that proves is that arguments based on authority are inductive. However, it is entirely reasonable to assume that the CFO is correct in their analysis because they are the Chief Financial Officer, and if any person knows, then it should be this person.

3. Analogies are the most helpful tool in our intellectual tool bag. Analogies are not only used in Logic, but they are also used in literally every discipline. Most of us are familiar with the rubber sheet analogy used by Einstein. He said that we should imagine holding a taunt rubber sheet, and then place a bowling ball in the center. The massive ball would make the middle of the sheet sink down. Now, if we took a handful of billiard balls and began to roll them across the sheet the balls would behave in a very particular way. The billiard balls would circle the bowling ball while gradually moving toward the center with the bowling ball. Einstein wants us to imagine that this is analogous to gravitational pull. The behavior that we can imagine on the rubber sheet is quite similar to the behavior of planets orbiting around the sun. The inference is merely probabilistic depending on the similarities between the two things.

    CNN reported that there was a mass shooting that occurred in Florida yesterday. Since media sources are conveying information about events occurring around the world, it follows that Fox News reported a similar story.

4. Arguments based on signs are to be taken quite literally. This is when the conclusion depends on a claim made on a sign. We should readily agree that not all signs are entirely trustworthy. Some signs are more reliable than others. Again, this only shows us that an argument based on a sign is inductive, and not that it is unreliable.

    The sign outside of the Palace of Versailles says that King Louis XIV moved the royal court from Paris in 1682. Therefore, we must conclude that he did indeed move the court in 1682.

    It is not hard to imagine a scenario in which the sign is not entirely accurate. A misprint, a disgruntled employee, a mistake in translation, or fabrications during the Enlightenment Era are all possible, but not probable.

5. The causal inference is the most common of all the inductive forms. Causation is the primary inference used in science. It occurs when the argument depends on a claim from a cause to an anticipated effect, or from an effect to an antecedent cause.

    The driver-side window of my car was smashed out last night, and my change cup is missing.

Therefore, a person broke into my car and stole some items.

My son is planning on jumping off the top of the house in hopes that he can fly like Peter Pan.

Therefore, I must stop him before he breaks some bones.

The former is an example of reasoning from the effect to the antecedent cause, and the latter is reasoning from the cause to the anticipated effect (mainly attempting to stop the effect from occurring).

e. Deductive forms

1. Deductive inferences and mathematics go hand in hand with one another. So, the first deductive form to recognize is an argument based on mathematics. This involves arguments in which the conclusion depends on measuring or computing in basic algebra and geometry. This does not include all types of mathematics though. Higher theoretical mathematics may be of the inductive type, specifically if induction proves it. Statistics is not deductive either. The nature of statistics is mere probability, so it is inductive. Look at the following example below:

   This triangle has two angles that are each 45 degrees.

   All triangles have 180 degrees.

   Therefore, the other angle of this triangle is 90 degrees.

2. Analytic definitions are true in virtue of their definitions. In other words, when the conclusion follows merely from the definition of a term in the premises, the argument is based on an analytic definition. Arguments of this type tend to be what Kant calls "trivial and uninformative," but they still follow with strict necessity.[4]

   My philosophy professor is cantankerous.

   Therefore, they are argumentative, standoffish, and disagreeable.

3. The next three forms are all syllogisms. The word "syllogism" denotes a type of argument in which there are two premises and exactly one conclusion. Each time that you encounter a syllogism, you will always have two premises and one conclusion. We are going to focus on three types of syllogisms in this next section.

   The first type is a categorical syllogism. We use the word "categorical" to refer to categories or domains in which a class is being related to another class. A categorical syllogism contains words like "All," "No," and "Some." Think back to the example that Aristotle created in antiquity.

---

[4] Kant, Immanuel and Norman K. Smith. *Immanuel Kant's Critique of Pure Reason*. Boston: Bedford, 1929. Print.

All men are mortal.

Socrates is a man.

Therefore, Socrates is a mortal.

In order to be classified as a categorical syllogism not all of the statements need to begin with "All," "No," or "Some." The example from Aristotle only contains one, and yet it is still a categorical syllogism. One could easily construct an argument in which all statements begin with a categorical quantifier.

All cats are mammals.

All mammals are animals.

Therefore, all cats are animals.

The second type is a disjunctive syllogism. In ordinary English, conjunction brings two simple statements together utilizing an "and." A disjunction, then, disjoins two simple statements, which allows them to be independent of one another. In ordinary English, we denote a disjunction with an "or" statement.

Either this class will be exhilarating, or it will be a nightmare.

This class is not exhilarating.

Therefore, this class is a nightmare.

If you are given two options, and one of them is not possible, then it follows with certainty that the other one must be the case.

The third type is a hypothetical syllogism. A hypothetical is a "what if" scenario. Hypothetical scenarios are the basis for Science-fiction, but in logic, a hypothetical is also known as a conditional. A hypothetical syllogism, much like a categorical syllogism, only needs one conditional in order to be classified as a hypothetical syllogism, but can have more.

If it is raining, then the sidewalks are wet.

It is raining.

Therefore, the sidewalks are wet.

An argument with only one conditional statement is called a "mixed hypothetical syllogism;" whereas an argument with three conditional statements is called a pure hypothetical syllogism.

Exercise 3.2

3.2.1 *Directions:* Determine whether the following arguments are inductive or deductive:

1. All Christians are monotheists. Some theists are not monotheists. Therefore, some theists are not Christians.
2. Historians have argued that it was the involvement in WWII that ended the Great Depression. Therefore, it probably follows that this did end the Great Depression.
3. We should either hire a new employee or terminate the position. The company would be worse off if we terminate the position. Therefore, we should hire a new employee.
4. The dining room is 20 ft. by 30 ft. Therefore, we should purchase 600 sq. ft. of flooring.
5. In the past, the droughts that occur in the summertime lead to forest fires. Therefore, it is reasonable to conclude that this summer will have forest fires.
6. The first-day handout says that we will have our first exam next week. So, we can expect our exam to occur next week.

*7. At Macomb Community College, 85% of the students who attend earn degrees. Therefore, it is very likely that if you begin your degree, then you will finish it.

8. If we attend work conferences, then we will earn certifications. If we earn certifications, then our pay will increase. It must be the case that if we attend work conferences, then our pay will increase.
9. Mount Masaya is continually emitting copious amounts of sulfur dioxide. Each year, tourists from all over the globe come to visit this site. Therefore, it is likely that people have been inhaling the sulfur dioxide.
10. The sign reads, "Road construction over the next two miles." Thus, we can expect to see the road construction occurring over the next two miles.

3.2.2 *Directions:* Indicate whether the following statements are true or false:

1. All arguments that follow out of necessity are inductive.
2. If an argument is based upon statistics, then it is deductive.
3. Causal arguments proceed from the knowledge of a cause to the knowledge of an effect, and vice versa.
4. A categorical syllogism is a deductive argument.
5. If an authority claims something to be true, then it must necessarily be true.

6. An argument that reasons from a small sample to an entire group in a deductive argument.
7. Inductive arguments are based entirely upon the supposition that what happened in the past will continue to happen in the future.
8. The word "syllogism" means two premises and one conclusion.
9. Deductive arguments conclude more than what is contained in the premises.
10. Inductive arguments only conclude what is contained in the premises.

f. Validity, Soundness, Strength, Cogency

1. Validity is referring to the internal structure of a deductive argument. Validity does not come in degrees. Hence, an argument is said to be valid or invalid. Think of validity as a light switch, mainly that it is a dichotomy between two exhaustive possibilities. There are two senses in which people use the word "valid." One is when people, often casually, say that is a "valid point," when they mean that it was a "good," "valuable," or "true" point. This is not the sense in which logicians use the word "valid." In logic, "valid" has a definite meaning that is intimately connected with structure. An argument is said to be valid, if and only if, it is impossible for the conclusion to be false, given that the premises are true. In other words, if the premises are true, then the conclusion must be true. It is important to note that just because the premises entail the truth of the conclusion does not mean that the premises and/or the conclusion are true. Validity does not have anything to do with the actual truth of the claims. It is merely expressing the relation between the premises and the conclusion. For instance, have a look at the two examples below:

   All professors are superheroes.

   Saul is a professor.

   Therefore, Saul is a superhero.

   All professors are superheroes.

   Saul is a superhero.

   Therefore, Saul is a professor.

   These arguments appear to be very similar, and in fact, many people may be inclined to say you can infer both of those conclusions. However, there is a fundamental difference between the two of them. We begin the test of validity by assuming the premises are true. Then we ask ourselves, "Is there an interpretation in which the premises are true, and the conclusion is false?" If there is no interpretation in which this is possible, then the argument is valid. If there is an interpretation in which this is possible, then the argument is invalid.

   Look at the first example. Without an inkling toward the actual truth of the premises and conclusion, go ahead and assume that the premises are true. Assuming that "All professors are superheroes," and "Saul is a professor," does it necessarily follow that "Saul is a superhero"? One should immediately recognize that it does necessarily follow from the premises. Thus, it is impossible for both of the premises to be true and the conclusion false. So, the argument is valid.

   Look at the second example. Again, put the issue of actual truth aside when testing the validity. Assuming that the premises are true, is it possible for the conclusion to be false? You will immediately recognize that it is possible for the conclusion to be false, given that the premises are true. Hence, the argument is invalid. Assuming that it is true that "All professors are superheroes" it does not follow from this that "All superheroes are professors." In other words, it is possible for there to be superheroes who are not professors, though it is not possible for there to be professors who are not superheroes as is stated in the premise. The second premise is that "Saul is a superhero," and then concludes from these two premises that "Saul is a professor." Even though we assume premise 1 is true, and that premise 2 is true, the truth of those premises does not necessitate the truth of the conclusion. So, there is an interpretation such that the premises are true and the conclusion is false, and that by definition, is an invalid argument. So, validity has to do with purported truth and their relationship to the conclusion, and not with the actual truth of the claims.

2. *Soundness* has to do with the actual truth of the premises. This is the final step of testing an argument. In fact, logic is not exclusively concerned with soundness. The truth or falsity of the claims is not determined by logic alone. This is where you will go outside of the realm of logic to establish the actual truth.

   An argument is said to be sound, if and only if, a set of conditions are satisfied. First of all, the argument must be deductive to be considered sound. Second, the argument must be valid. So, if the argument is not valid, then it cannot be sound. Lastly, the argument must have all true premises. There is a caveat for the last condition. The condition of *all true premises* must have some inferential connection leading to the conclusion. The addition of one superfluous false premise does not make the argument unsound. Look at the example below:

   All cats are animals.

   Garfield is a cat.

   No cats are fluffy.

   Therefore, Garfield is an animal.

   If you test the validity, you will recognize that it is impossible for the conclusion to be false, given that the premises are true. So, the argument is valid. When testing the soundness, you will recognize that premises 1 and 2 are actually true, whereas premise 3 is false. This does not make the argument unsound though. That is since the premise "No cats are fluffy" is not only false, but it also has not inferential connection to the other premises.

   An argument is unsound when the argument is invalid or has one or more false premises, or both. To explain this a bit more, an argument that is invalid is automatically unsound.

   Remember that one of the necessary conditions for *soundness* is validity, so if it is not valid, then it is not sound. The argument could be valid but have one or more false premises(s) in which case it is unsound, or it could be both. Look at the following examples below:

   All men are mortal.

   Socrates is a mortal.

Therefore, Socrates is a man.

All professors are superheroes.

Saul is a professor.

Therefore, Saul is a superhero.

All professors are superheroes.

Saul is a superhero.

Therefore, Saul is a professor.

The first example has a poor structure. Assuming that the premises are true, it is possible for the conclusion to be false. This argument is invalid, and hence it is unsound. The second argument is appropriately structured. Assuming that the premises are true, it is not possible for the conclusion to be false. This argument is valid (satisfying the second condition), but the premises are not actually true (professors are not superheroes), so the argument is unsound. The third example has poor structure, and the premises are not true; thus it is unsound.

3. Validity and soundness pertain to deductive arguments. So, it would be inappropriate to use the same concepts for inductive arguments. With inductive arguments, logicians use strength and cogency. An argument is said to be strong if the conclusion follows with a high degree of probability. An argument is weak if the conclusion follows with a low degree of probability. Look at the following examples:

   In the past, the class has begun at 11 am on Monday and Wednesday.

   Therefore, this upcoming Wednesday class will begin at 11 am.

   Last night I received a text message at 1 am.

   Therefore, tonight I will receive a text message at 1 am.

   The first example is relying on induction from similar events that has happened in the past. Assuming that class has started at 11 am in the past, it is highly likely that it will continue to occur at that time. Since the argument is inductive, there is always a chance that it might not start at 11 am (flat tire, illness, email not delivered, and the like). However, the second example is relying on a fluke or random event to justify what will happen in the future. The fact that I received a text message one night does not allow one to infer that it will happen in the future. The premise is not strong enough to lead us to the conclusion, and so the argument is weak. Usually, the easiest way to distinguish between a strong and a weak argument is by the probability. If the conclusion follows with 49.99% likelihood or higher, the argument is strong. If the conclusion follows with 49.98% likelihood or lower, the argument is weak.

Logicians rely heavily upon the uniformity of nature to aid with this classification. As we have already discussed, the past tends to replicate in the future. Based on the many occurrences in the past, it is justified to assume that it will continue to occur in the future. It is indeed possible for it to not continue in the future though. Logicians recognize that those things that have happened many times in the past have a high likelihood to continue in the future, and things that don't have many occurrences in the past are not as likely to happen in the future. When you show up for a class at 11 am on Monday and Wednesday, you are doing so because every other time in the past, the class has met at 11 am. However, when a person sends you a text at 1 am, this is not an ongoing event in the past; thus we are not justified in assuming it will happen in the future.

David Hume, the Scottish philosopher, was one of the first to elaborate on the uniformity of nature. In the *Treatise of Human Nature*, Hume asks us to imagine a scenario in which your best friend tells you that they saw a statue cry over the weekend.[5] You have no reason to believe that your friend is lying to you. Why do you trust them? It is simple, induction. In the past, your friend has always been truthful. So, you think that because they have always told you the truth, they must be telling you the truth right now. Much like when a friend lies to you in the past, you are cautious about trusting them in the future. Hume says that if you are going to use induction to trust your friend about that statue crying, then you must use induction with the uniformity of nature. He says that "a wise person always proportions his beliefs to the available evidence."[6] Although perhaps you might be inclined to disagree with this general principle, I think it is the mark of prudence to act accordingly. Hume asks you to stack up all of the inductive evidence on both sides and ultimately side with the stronger inductive evidence. Hume says that the amount of times that your friend has told you the truth the past is in no way even remotely close to the amount of past evidence that statues do not cry. You have overwhelming evidence that statues do not cry (past induction) and you are being told by your friend to ignore all of that evidence for their testimony (contrary to the uniformity of nature). Nature has dictated, as far as we know, by past experience that statues do not cry. Hume asks, "Which is the greater inductive argument?" To this, we should all answer, the fact that statues do not cry. Hume says that "It would be more miraculous that your friend is lying to you or is acting out of self-deception than an actual miracle taking place."[7] For Hume owns, that "it is certainly possible that miracles occur… though it would be nearly impossible to find in all of history."[8] He is claiming that even though he grants it is possible that events which have not occurred in the past might actually occur in the future, our modes of knowing things (induction) forbids us from genuinely knowing these things. So, to understand the uniformity of nature is to accept those events that have happened repeatedly in the past, and to be skeptical of events that have not happened in the past.

---

[5] Hume, David, David F. Norton, and Mary J. Norton. *A Treatise of Human Nature*. Oxford: Oxford University Press, 2000. Print.

[6] *Ibid.*

[7] *Ibid.*

[8] *Ibid.*

Since induction and deduction are conceptually different, we do not use the concept of *soundness* for inductive arguments. Cogency is the last step in testing inductive arguments. For an argument to be cogent, it must be inductive, strong, and have all true premises. The same caveat applies to inductive arguments. It must be *all true premises* that have an inferential connection to the conclusion.

An argument is uncogent when the argument is weak or has one or more false premises, or both. To explain this a bit more, an argument that is weak is automatically unsound. Remember, one of the necessary conditions for *cogency* is that it must be strong, so if it is weak, then it is uncogent. The argument could be strong but have one or more false premises in which case it is uncogent, or it could be both. Look at the following examples below:

> Most of the students from England did poor on the calculus test.
>
> Therefore, students from England are bad at math.

> The Detroit News reported that a volcanic eruption occurred last night in Macomb County.
>
> The Detroit News is a reputable source.
>
> Therefore, a volcanic eruption did occur last night in Macomb County.

> Entire chariots were found at the bottom of the Red Sea.
>
> Many people in chariots attempted to cross the Red Sea when Moses split the waterway.
>
> Therefore, Moses did, in fact, split the Red Sea.

The first example is weak, and therefore, it is uncogent. Assuming that a group of students from England did poor on a calculus test does not mean that students from England are bad at math, that conclusion follows with a low degree of probability. The second example is strong. Assuming that the Detroit News reported the eruption and that it is a reputable source, it is highly likely that the eruption did, in fact, take place. However, the first premise is false. A volcanic eruption did not occur in Michigan. So, this argument is uncogent. The third example is both weak and has a false premise. Assuming that the premises are true, it only follows with a low degree of probability. The uniformity of nature is such that we have hardly any evidence of people splitting the sea in half with their will. It is also the case that the first premise is false. Chariots were not found at the bottom of the Red Sea.

Wakefield's Flow Chart of Truth

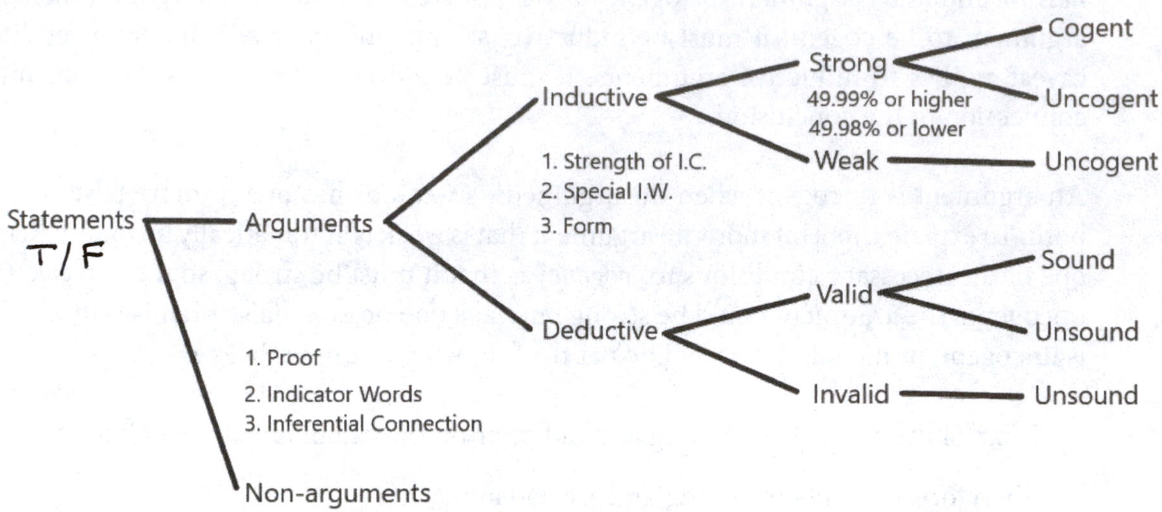

Figure created by Bradley Wakefield.

Exercise 3.3

3.3.1 *Directions:* Explain the following concepts. Write a few sentences explaining all of the necessary conditions of these concepts.

1. Soundness
2. Cogency
3. Validity
4. Strength

3.3.2 *Directions:* Indicate whether the following statements are true or false:

1. A valid argument can have false premises.
2. If the argument is invalid, then it is uncogent.
3. Philosophers use the uniformity of nature to help determine inductive inferences.
4. An argument with a false premise can still be cogent.
5. Validity and soundness can be determined simultaneously.
6. If an argument is strong, then it must be cogent.
7. The actual truth of the premises helps us determine the validity.
8. Validity comes in degrees.

3.3.3 *Directions:* Determine whether the following arguments are inductive or deductive. Once you have completed this, determine the validity or the strength of the argument.

1. Spanish is the most common language spoken in the world. Therefore, it is highly probable that someone is speaking Spanish right now.
2. According to the pamphlet handed out on the street, Africa is the largest continent. Therefore, it is the largest continent in the world.
3. If I write my term paper in advance, then I will have time to visit the Reading and Writing Studio. I did not write my term paper in advance. So, I will not have time to visit the Reading and Writing Studio.

*4. I recently purchased a swimming pool for my backyard. The pool is $18' \times 33' \times 4'$. Therefore, it must be the case that the pool holds 14,000 gallons of water.

5. My colleague gave me a surreptitious look at the conference last week. There must have been something hidden that they wanted me to realize.

6. Most universities require a letter of recommendation for admission. Therefore, I should probably find a person to write me a letter of recommendation.
7. All vehicles must pass specific emission standards. All SUVs must pass specific emission standards. It follows that all vehicles are SUVs.
8. Since Martin Luther sparked the Protestant Reformation in 1517, and 1517 was the middle of the Renaissance, it follows that the Protestant Reformation occurred during the Renaissance.
9. Someone created this book. Since everything that I have experienced has come from something, it follows that the universe came from something.
10. The majority of the U.S. experiences snowfall each year, therefore it is likely that Florida will experience snowfall this year.

g. Testing forms

1. In order to test the form of an argument, you must first be able to put the argument into its argument form. So, argument form is replacing the terms in an argument with symbolic letters (assignment of letters is arbitrary) to expose the internal structure of the argument. Look at the following argument below:

   All Democrats are politicians.

   All politicians are elected officials.

   Therefore, all Democrats are elected officials.

   If we replace the terms "democrats" with 'D,' "politicians" with 'P,' and "elected officials" with 'E,' then we will get the following form:

   (1) All D are P

   (2) All P are E

   ∴ All D are E

   This is the argument form of the preceding argument. This now shows the internal structure of the argument. When we test validity, we are checking to see if the internal structure is fine. If the structure is fine, then we can move onto to the actual truth of the premises, and if the structure is not fine, then there is no need to go any further for the argument is invalid, and thus unsound.

   In general, a counterexample is an example that is contrary to what the original example states. So, if we took the proposition "All crows are black" and we wanted a counterexample to this, we would only need to show one non-black crow. If "All crows are black," then there should be no crows that are non-black. So, when I can show at least one crow that is non-black, I have provided a counterexample. The same principle applies to arguments. If the internal structure is flawed, then I only need to show one example of the form not working. In logic, a flawed argument structure is an invalid argument. An invalid argument is such that it is possible for the conclusion to be false, given that the premises are true. When testing an argument form to see whether or not it is invalid, you will try to find at least one example of true premises leading to a false conclusion. Once you take the argument and reduce it to argument form, then you can begin the counterexample method. The counterexample method is substituting the symbolic letters with simple terms to prove the form invalid. The following list may be used as simple terms to prove the form invalid:

Dogs
Cats
Fish
Animals
Mammals

No rudimentary principles are complex, and some axiomatic suppositions are not complex; therefore, all axiomatic suppositions are rudimentary principles.

(1) No R are C	R: Dogs
(2) Some A are not C	A: Fish
∴ All A are R	C: Cats

(T) No dogs are cats.

(T) Some fish are not cats.

(F) ∴ All fish are dogs.

Another way to explain the counterexample method is to compare it to proofreading a term paper. Suppose that you are evaluating a paragraph to see if it is well written. We know that a paragraph is a collection of sentences. So, the well-written paragraph is dependent upon well-written sentences. If I were to find one well-written sentence, then I am not able to say that the whole paragraph is well written. That is, one well-written sentence is only one small part of the whole paragraph and is not enough to speak on behalf of the entire paragraph. However, if I found one sentence that is not well written, then I can condemn the entire paragraph. If the paragraph is a collection of sentences, then one poorly written sentence would allow us to deny that the whole paragraph is well written. So, the counterexample method is essentially adhering to the same process. Look for an interpretation in which the premises are true and the conclusion is false much like looking for a poorly written sentence. Once you find such an instance, then you may classify the argument as invalid. If there is no instance of that, then the argument is valid.

Exercise 3.4

3.4.1 *Directions:* Put the following arguments into argument form. Once you have completed this, then perform a substitution instance on each argument form to prove it invalid, that is, counterexample method. To prove the form invalid, please select terms from the following list: cat, dog, fish, animal, and mammal.

1. Some fans of fiction are not Star Wars fans, and all Star Wars fans are fans of science fiction. It follows that some fans of fiction are fans of science fiction.
2. All reality stars are egotistical. For some Hollywood actors are egotistical, and all reality stars are Hollywood actors.
3. Some genetically modified organisms are not products harmful to the consumer. Thus, since some genetically modified organisms are cheaper to produce, some products harmful to the consumer are not cheaper to produce.
4. Some extraterrestrials are not human-like in form. Some extraterrestrials are anthropomorphic deities. Therefore, some anthropomorphic deities are human-like in form.
5. No farmers are Wall Street executives. Since some farmers are millionaires and some Wall Street executives are not millionaires.
6. All professional wrestling events are scripted beforehand. Therefore, because no professional wrestling events are sporting events, no sporting events are scripted beforehand.
7. No member of the American Philosophical Association are physicists, and no member of the American Philosophical Association are scientists, it follows that no scientists are physicists.
8. No space shuttles are permanent residencies. All free-floating entities are space shuttles. No permanent residencies are free-floating entities.
9. All detectives are police officers, and no police officers are sleuths. It follows with certainty that all sleuths are detectives.
10. Some Tarot card readers are charlatans. Thus, since no magicians are Tarot card readers, all magicians are charlatans.

SECTION IV

Informal Logic

a. What is language?

1. Aristotle says that we first begin by experiencing certain phenomena in the world. Once we have had an experience, we would like to share that experience.[1] Most people are interested in sharing that experience instead of keeping it to themselves. Aristotle says that language is meant to express our ideas of particular phenomena. So, language and our experiences are intimately connected. However, language cannot do anything whatsoever. There are constraints on language. Aristotle believes that to be the primary function of logic. Logic constrains not only what language can express, but also limits our ideas. In order for language to function correctly, we must understand how to *use* language effectively.

2. *Words, concepts*, and *referents* are the starting point in this section. Let us begin this section with *referents*. The *referents* are the individual things out in the world. For example, if you are reading this text, then you are familiar with a *referent*. This particular textbook is a *referent*. It is an object demarcated from other objects in the world with boundaries and has specific features. So, if the *referent* is the particular thing in the world, then other things that are very similar to this thing is part of a broader class of things. We call this a *concept*.

   A *concept* is an idea that stands for a broader class of things. The *concept* of a book includes all of the *referents* that belong to this *concept*. There are many books, some small, large, old, new, literary, scientific, etc. Although there are differences among them, they all share one thing in

[1] Aristotle, Owen F. Octavius, and Porphyry. *The Organon, or Logical Treatises, of Aristotle*. London: G. Bell and Sons, 1883. Print.

common, mainly they all belong to the class of books. The class of books is a grouping of all the particular books that exist. Though each book may be different in certain respects, there is something fundamental to all books that make them different from other objects. We call these "essential properties." The aim here is not to establish the essential properties of what makes a thing a thing—a concern for other areas of philosophy—it is important to acquaint yourself with these distinctions. Rather, we will take an ordinary language approach in this text and try to establish some of the overlapping criteria for each concept. In philosophy, this is known as a conceptual analysis.

Lastly, we then look at a *word*. A *word* is a group of symbols used to express an idea. If we were in front of a *referent,* then we could continually talk about that *referent* by merely pointing to it. Once we are no longer in front of that *referent*, we would have a hard time referring to it. Thus, language is meant as a sort of label to talk about things that are not immediately in front of us. The *word* and the *referent* is a connection that is not necessary. Take, for example, the word "tree." The *referent* is the thing protruding from the ground, with branches, leaves, roots, etc. That thing is clearly distinguished from other things, like a flower for example. However, the *referent* and the *word* are not necessarily connected. The *word* "tree" has no necessary connection to the *referent*. We could have originally called a *tree* a *schmee* and still retained the same meaning. This is same with other languages referring to the same thing. "Fenetre" and "window" are referring to the same *referent*. However, the former is in French, and the latter is in English. In this sense, *words* are arbitrary, but *concepts* are not. The *concept* of a tree is not some random assignment of *referents* where we merely or accidentally included all the parts of the *referent*. The *concept* includes all of the essential properties that make it that particular thing. *Words* are not the same. *Words* are merely arbitrary assignments of symbols that are then attached to the *referents* and *concepts*.

3. Since *concepts* are grouping similar *referents* together, there is a hierarchy among *concepts*. Aristotle used a few terms to classify the hierarchy of *concepts*. He used *genus* and *species*—terms that have now been adopted in Biology. Genus is the broad sense in which we group concepts, and species is the narrow sense in which we group concepts. In this way, the usage of "genus" and "species" is somewhat fluid. For example, the concept of animal is a *genus*, mainly because it includes all of the classes of things that make up the *concept*. Under this *genus* is the class of dogs, cats, hamsters, horses, etc. Each of those classes is comprised of sets of *referents* or *species*. The *species* is the set of all dogs, the set of all cats, and so on. In my office, I have a file cabinet. The file cabinet is divided into the *genus* of Introduction to Philosophy, Logic, Ethics, Professional Ethics, and Philosophy of Religion. Each drawer is the *genus*, and once you open each drawer, you will find a *species*. These are the folders that include all of the information for each section of Logic—section 1, 2, 3, and 4. The *genus* and *species* distinction are fluid because you can zoom in or out to classify *concepts*. For example, you could say that the file is the *genus* and that the particular paper in the file is the *species*. I have a folder named, "Exams," which includes all of the exams for the entire Logic course. So, the folder (*genus*) is a set of all of the exams (*species*).

Exercise 4.1

4.1.1 *Directions:* Indicate whether the following statements are true or false:

1. The *genus* is the narrow sense of grouping together similar objects.
2. *Words* are necessarily connected to their *referents.*
3. A *referent* is an individual object of perception found in the world.
4. The hierarchy of concepts has been most often used in Biology.
5. All *concepts* are a collection of words.
6. *Words* are symbols used to refer to objects when we are not immediately in front of them.
7. *Species* and *genus* are a way of grouping similar objects together.
8. *Referents* may have more than only one symbol to refer to it.

4.1.2 *Directions:* Please review the following passage below. Then, describe how a *word, referent,* and *concept* are being used in the passage.

Example:

CASSIUS: Did Cicero say anything?

CASCA: Ay, he spoke Greek.

CASSIUS: To what effect?

CASCA: Nay, an I tell you that, I'll ne'er look you i' th' face again. But those that understood him smiled at one another and shook their heads. But, for mine own part, it was Greek to me. I could tell you more news too. Murellus and Flavius, for pulling scarfs off Caesar's images, are put to silence. Fare you well. There was more foolery yet, if I could remember it.[2]

Word—The words being used are in Greek. Casca does not speak this language and is not sure what the words are referring to. This was done to deliberately confuse some of the listeners.

Referent—Cassius is using the words to as a vehicle to refer to a particular event. Thus, whether it is in Greek or English, the same thing is being denoted.

---

[2] Shakespeare, William, Barbara A. Mowat, and Paul Werstine. *The Tragedy of Julius Caesar.* New York: Washington Square Press, 2005. Print.

Concept—The set of referents denoted with a certain type of symbols that make up a language. In this case, the type of symbols is known as the conceptual understanding of the Greek language.

1. JULIET: Tis but thy name that is my enemy;
   Thou art thyself, though not a
   Montague.
   What's Montague? It is nor hand,
   nor foot,
   Nor arm, nor face, nor any other
   Part
   Belonging to a man. O, be some
   Other name!
   What's in a name? that which we
   call a rose
   By any other name would smell as
   sweet;
   So Romeo would, were he not
   Romeo call'd,
   Retain that dear perfection which
   he owes
   Without that title. Romeo, doff thy
   name,
   And for that name which is no part of thee
   Take all myself. (2.2.38–49)[3]

[3] Shakespeare, William, and Alan Durband. *Romeo and Juliet*. Woodbury, NY: Barron's, 1985. Print.

b. Language games

1. Twentieth-century philosopher, Ludwig Wittgenstein, proposed that many philosophical problems arise from issues with language.[4] He is part of what is known as the "Linguistic turn" in philosophy. This is a dynamic shift in the focus of philosophy from epistemic concerns to linguistic concerns. Wittgenstein realized that language could function in many different ways. Language does not always have a straightforward literal approach. That is, language can function as story-telling, irony, double entendre, a figure of speech, euphemism, etc. Wittgenstein thought that before you can reasonably evaluate a person's ideas, you must first understand which language game the person is playing. For example, after a squabble with a significant other, you might say "I always help you with chores," when, in fact, you do not literally mean that. You probably mean something like, "I occasionally help you with things around the house." Another example is when we say, "I am starving to death," which is clearly a hyperbole. You mean that you are very hungry; however, you exaggerate to emphasize your point. He recognizes that much of philosophy has been the same way. Philosophers have been talking around one another, which had made solutions to philosophical problems delayed if not impossible.

2. Though there are many ways in which language can function, two primary functions are essential to the introductory student. That is *emotive* and *cognitive* functions. The *emotive* function does just as the name suggests, it focuses on the emotions of the reader/listener. The *emotive* function is to elicit as many emotions possible from the reader/listener in order to get that person to accept their claims. On the other hand, the *cognitive* function does just as the name suggests, it focuses on the cognition of the reader/listener. Here, the goal is to present the reader/listener with facts and information that support the person's hypothesis. The *cognitive* function has no tricks, games, or levels of deception. When one takes the *cognitive* approach, that person knows that the facts and their arrangement are strong enough to convince the reader/listener of the hypothesis without any rhetoric. Look at the following examples below:

    King Louis XVI and Queen Marie Antoinette were the monarchs of France until the French Revolution of 1792. They were staying at the Palace of Versailles during the Revolution. Locals rushed the Palace seizing the King and Queen and imprisoning them in Paris until they abolished the monarchy and executed them in 1793.

    The cowardly and purely academic monarch, King Louis XVI, did not have the control over his people like his predecessors. His weak chin and childish attitude lead him to be executed by the local people of France. As the locals grew contempt for the lazy and arrogant ruler, a revolution started to brew. King Louis XVI and his wife, Queen Marie Antoinette, were dragged from their palace to Paris only to be brutally murdered by a guillotine execution. The blood-hungry mob insisted that their heads be removed to put them on a spike then and pass them around the crowds like a team celebrating with a trophy.

---

[4] Wittgenstein, Ludwig and G. E. M. Anscombe. *Philosophical Investigations*. Oxford, UK: Blackwell, 1997. Print.

The former is merely conveying information about the execution of King Louis XVI, whereas the latter is appealing to emotions. It is saying harsh and negative things about King Louis XVI and the mob. The former does not possess a positive or negative attitude toward the event. It is merely presenting the facts. Because of this, the reader/listener can collect all of the facts of the event. The latter is not so easily completed. Because there is a bunch of emotional language, it is hard for the reader/listener to pull out the facts. The facts are masqueraded with an emotional appeal.

When we make the judgment that something is good/bad, right/wrong, permissible/impermissible, acceptable/unacceptable, we are imposing value in the claim. The value of a claim can be either positive or negative. We should recognize that if you are going to impose a negative or positive value on something, then you need proof for that. The proof must lie outside of the emotion that I can elicit from the reader/listener. For, if the reader/listener does not demand evidence for the value judgment, then the emotive rhetoric will appear as though it is proper evidence. When I say, "Eating meat is wrong," I am expressing a negative attitude toward the consumption of animal products. After I express this proposition, you should immediately ask, "Why is eating meat wrong?" You want an argument to defend the hypothesis. It is not enough to say that *it is* wrong. It is also equally wrong to appeal to emotive functions. For example, "Poor and innocent little animals are dragged from their cages to be hung upside down and savagely beaten to death only to add another layer to your already loaded hamburger" is using the emotive function. Although this is saying something negative about meat consumption, it is not defending why it is wrong. Its only function here is to elicit emotions from the reader/listener in hopes that his alone with changing their mind about meat consumption.

Why would someone use the *emotive* function instead of the preferred cognitive function? Well, I think that there are a few reasons why that is done. First involves the difficulty in constructing an argument. This is akin to putting a scientific study together. This can be long, daunting, and easily mistaken. Thus, some people do not have the time nor the ability to construct a good argument with facts, an inferential connection, and well thought-out claims. In this sense, some people are cognitively inept. The second reason as to why people use *emotive* function is because they are disinclined to work harder than they deem necessary. Some people are lazy and look for the easiest way to complete a task. What is the point of carefully constructing claims, with an inferential connection, and a natural succession of ideas, when they could use the natural default position? Their emotions motivate most people over reason. Charlotte Bronte famously once said, "Better to be without logic than without feeling."[5] This proverb is intimately connected with most of humanity. If it is already widely accepted that feelings guide us through life, then it is no wonder why many people think that using *emotive* function is much more effective than *cognitive* function. Philosophers prefer *cognitive* over *emotive* because they would rather not have to sift through all of the *emotive* claims to extrapolate the value judgment. It is easier to establish the truth of *cognitive* claims than it is for *emotive* claims. Since logic is concerned with statements, *cognitive* claims are a better fit.

[5] Bronte, Charlotte. *The Professor.* Chapter XXIV. Smith, Elder & Co. 1857.

Exercise 4.2

4.2.1 *Directions:* Determine whether the following passages contain emotive or cognitive meaning.

1. A pit-bull is a vicious creature who is entirely unsafe for young children to be around.
2. A pit-bull has a strong bite that is only released when it wants to.
3. Government officials are only pandering to voters to get re-elected and serve their selfish desires through corporate interests.
4. Government officials are elected officials who are meant to serve on behalf of their voters. Their power is bestowed upon them by the people who elected them.
5. My significant other was a drug addict, who was abusive and threatening to me. I was forced to file a police report about such issues.
6. My significant other is a crazy sociopath. They get this look in their eye that makes me shiver. I should have the police arrest them.

*7. My European vacation was so amazing and wonderful. Each day was more incredible than the previous day.

8. My European vacation was very informative. We visited historical sites, which provided an in-depth analysis of each event. We were able to return with a wealth of information.
9. "Crooked Hilary" was involved in a uranium deal that was a quid pro quo for large donations to the Clinton Foundation.
10. Hilary Clinton was one of nine people to sit on the committee overseeing the transaction of Uranium One. In fact, she did not have the legal authority to veto the transaction either.

c. Unclear meaning

1. "Ambiguity: the devil's volleyball."[6] Ambiguity has to do with multiple meanings. A term is said to be ambiguous if there are multiple clear meanings. It must be noted that each of those meanings is clearly understood. For example, "bank," "light," "chest," "gay," "happy," "bat," "club," and "sign" are all ambiguous. When we use the word "bank," we are using it in one or more senses that are established in the language. "Bank" could mean: (i) a riverbank, (ii) financial institution, or (iii) a bank turn in an aircraft. Each of these meanings though is easily apprehended. It should be quite apparent that when creating an argument, that you should make sure to use terms in the same sense throughout the entire argument. Arguments that use terms in a different sense throughout are committing a fallacy (Equivocation), which will be discussed in the section on informal fallacies.

2. Vagueness is not the same as ambiguity. Sometimes people will say that a term or statement is vague when they mean uninformative. If I were to ask you how many people are in the room and you respond, "More than three and fewer than hundred" you are being uninformative or lacking specificity. That is not to say, you are being vague though. Vagueness has to do with borderline cases in which it is not clear whether or not the term applies. Which number of hairs on a person's head would make him or her bald? What is the minimum height to be counted as tall? These questions and a plethora of others are meant to show the absurdity of vagueness. Vagueness has to do with our ignorance of meaning. With ambiguity, we know all of the multiple meanings, but with vagueness, we are not sure of the meaning. So, if we are not sure of the meaning, then we will have a hard time establishing when to apply or deny an application of a term. If a term is vague, we can think of its definition as being a bit blurred or fuzzy. Think about the word "bald" for a moment. It is not clear when we should apply the word "bald" to a person. Some may be inclined to say that a person with "zero hairs is bald." Anything more than zero hairs and the person is not bald. Suppose that a person only had one hair on their head, but this is unbeknownst to you. You would say that the person is bald, when in fact, they are not. Even if we assign the definition of zero hairs to the concept of bald, we are still subject to the problems of vagueness. A person may have just shaved their head making it appear as though they are bald, but the hairs are too short to see with the naked eye. So, you say that the person is bald, but they have millions of tiny hairs that you cannot see. If we stipulated the word "bald" to a certain number of hairs, then you would need to count the hairs before classifying the person as bald—a long tedious and arduous task. Thus, in both situations, you are saying something that is false. The amount of hairs used to determine whether or not a person is bald is only one sense of the word "bald." Terms can be vague and ambiguous though not used synonymously.

3. When we think of baldness, we are also thinking of coverage. The amount of coverage on a person's head seems to, in part, constitute baldness. Suppose that a person has one large hair follicle (5-inch diameter) and that hair is directly on top of their head. Although most of the

[6] Phillips, Emo. https://twitter.com/EmoPhilips?lang=en. Accessed 31 Mar. 2016.

head is covered, the person only has one hair and is technically not bald. Similarly, suppose that a person has hardly any coverage on their head, but numerically they are not bald. In the back of their head is a large group of hairs. There are one million hairs contained in the size of a quarter. In this case, they have the numbers, but they do not have the coverage. Is the person bald or not? This also brings up an interesting point. Another essential aspect of baldness is the location of hairs. Where does my head end and my neck begin? It appears as though the word "head" is vague. If I have a bunch of hairs that are on my neck, then I would be bald, but if those hairs are on my head, then I am not bald.

When you ask someone, "Well that depends on what you mean by such and such?" it usually signifies that the person is using a term that is vague or ambiguous and that a further definition is needed to resolve the issue.

4. Sorites Paradox arises from the problem of vagueness. The word "Soros" means heap. So, the Sorites Paradox is the problem of the heap. If we begin with a plausible premise that "a person with 100 million dollars is rich" and subtract one dollar at a time, and one increment cannot make the difference between rich and not rich, then it appears we will inevitably come to the absurd conclusion that "a person with zero dollars is rich." The Sorites Paradox is constructed from vague predicates in a proposition, whereas seemingly true premises and impeccable logical reasoning leads to a false conclusion. *Modus ponens* is the valid rule of inference used in the following version of a Sorites Paradox:

   Base step: A person with zero hairs is bald.

   Inductive Premise: If n hairs on a person's head are enough to make that person bald, and one hair cannot make a difference between bald and non-bald, then so are $n + 1$ hairs.

   Conclusion: A person with 100,000 hairs is bald.[7]

   Some may think that vagueness is merely a problem with language and that stipulation can resolve this issue. However, it should become apparent that the stipulation would not help the problem of vagueness. Think about the word "tall" for a moment. If we were to stipulate the word "tall," then we would have to provide an adequate definition that would solve any case of vagueness. Think about what that would entail. "Tall" can be applied to people, flowers, buildings, and insects, and so on. Let's focus on people for a moment. We might be inclined to say that anyone who is 6 inches is tall. Thus, we would again have the problem of pulling out a measuring tape for borderline cases. There is also a perceptive problem as well. The person who is only a millimeter shorter than 6 inches would appear to the naked eye as 6 inches and hence *tall*, but in reality, this person is not 6 inches and hence not *tall*. The stipulation would need to include all the possibilities of *tall* for a person. The predicate "tall" may be applied to

[7] Wakefield, Bradley. *Trivalency in a Contextual Penumbra: An Alternative Solution to the Sorites Paradox*. Wayne State University, 2014. Print.

men, women, children, adolescent, elder, basketball player, horse jockey, and even certain ethnicities. Imagine trying to account for all of the possibilities of "tallness"? It would be nearly impossible. It would be an endless endeavor to think that you could resolve the issue of vagueness by stipulation.

Even if we were successful in stipulating the definition of "tall" we still have not solved the problem of vagueness. Objects are vague. This is not just a problem with language; it is a problem with fuzzy boundaries. For example, a baseball is vague. It is hard to imagine that one atom could make the difference between a baseball and a non-baseball. Suppose I took a baseball and removed one atom, does a baseball remain? If you answer in the negative, then you are stuck in the very unsavory position of saying that the removal of a small piece changes the object. If I took a book and removed one page, it would be absurd to say that it is no longer a book. If you say that the removal of one atom from the baseball does not change the baseball into a non-baseball, then the paradox is established. If one atom cannot make the difference, then I can repeatedly remove one atom at a time, thus making no significant change of the object from baseball to a non-baseball. I will continue this removal for a long stretch of time until eventually, I conclude that "zero atoms is a baseball' a patently false claim to make. The problem of vagueness (Sorites Paradox) was established in antiquity and was not revived until the beginning of the twentieth century. The problem resurfaces with the advancement of science. Science is out to explain phenomena with exactitude and precision. The problem, though, is the language with which we use to explain the phenomena. If language is vague, then how can science use this vague language for exactitude? It appears as though for there to be any success in scientific literature, we must first dismantle Sorites Paradox and the problem of vagueness.

Exercise 4.3

4.3.1 *Directions:* Indicate whether the following statements are true or false:

1. Vagueness and ambiguity are essentially the same.
2. Ambiguity involves multiple clear meanings.
3. The word "bald" is vague because it is not clear when the term is correctly applied.
4. The sorites paradox can be solved by stipulating definitions for vague terms.
5. Some terms are vague and ambiguous.
6. Only terms are vague.
7. Definitions help with problems of ambiguity.
8. The sorites paradox is the little by little argument.
9. Context can help resolve the problems of vagueness.
10. In the twentieth century, vagueness was revived from the advancements in science.

4.3.2 *Directions:* The following terms are both vague and ambiguous. Please briefly explain how they may be expressed as being vague and ambiguous and provide an example.

Example: *Light*. The word "light" can be both vague and ambiguous. It is ambiguous because it could mean making things visible, electromagnetic radiation, or of little weight. It is also vague because if we think that something is "light" being that it is of little weight, then it is not clear when that particular thing becomes light. Suppose we start with something that is heavy and remove a very tiny section at a time. We will not be able to discern when the object is no longer heavy and is hence light.

Red *Sound* *Bat*

d. Denotation versus Connotation

1. A *term* is a word or a group of words that is designating something. Usually, that something being designated is the subject of a proposition. A term includes descriptive phrases, proper names, and common names. You can talk about the word itself, or you can use in its ordinary sense. When you speak about the word itself, it is essential to put the word in quotation marks. That way, the reader knows that you are referring to the word as a symbol and not using it. When I say, "'Cat' has three letters," I am uttering a proposition that is not only true, it is also mentioning the word "cat" and not using it. However, when I say, "Cats are creepy," I am uttering a proposition that may be true, but more importantly, is it using the word "cat" not mentioning it. If you use a word and mention the same word, then both of those instances are terms. That is, they are both serving as the subject of a proposition.

2. Connotation and denotation are both parts of the meaning of the term. When we think of the word "cat," this includes both the qualities that make the thing a cat, but we are also speaking of those objects that move around the world in certain sorts of ways. So, there are qualities of a cat, and there are things that are cats. The former is speaking of the *connotation* of the term. The terms "connotation," "sense," and "intensional" may be used interchangeably. So, we should think of connotation as the qualities that make the term what it is. The latter is *denotation* that includes all of the members of that class of objects. The terms "denotation," "reference," and "extensional" may be used interchangeably. As mentioned earlier, Aristotle claims that objects have essential qualities that make it what it is. In this section, we are not concerned with the *necessary* qualities that make a thing what it is. We are more so concerned with qualities that are *usually* attributed to a thing. For example, we often describe an animal by saying, "It has four legs, and sharp teeth, etc.," however, having four legs is not essential to a thing being what it is. It is indeed possible for there to be a cat that does not have any legs at all, and yet, it is still a cat.

   It is the connotation that helps us determine the denotation. The more specific the connotation, the more specific the denotation (concrete). The broader the connotation, the broader the denotation (abstract). It must be stated, that all terms have at least connotation, but not all have denotation. That is, not all objects are classes or things out in the world. However, in order for that thing to be conceptualized, it must have some qualities to it. For without qualities, you are not able to think of anything. Although Santa Claus does not exist, or better yet, does not have denotation, Santa still has connotation. Unicorns, Leprechauns, and even the current King of France has connotation, though none of these objects will have denotation. If the terms have connotation and no denotation, these terms are part of the empty set. The empty set is the set of objects that has no members. Terms that are part of the empty set have either been in the empty set forever, or they once had denotation and no longer have it—current King of France.

Exercise 4.4

4.4.1 *Directions:* Indicate whether the following statements are true or false:

1. Intension determines the extension of a term.
2. A term may have empty intension.
3. The empty extension is only for imaginary objects.
4. The extension of a term is all of the members of the class.
5. The intension is the qualities that make a thing what it is.
6. A term is always the predicate of the statement.
7. Mentioning a term is using it in the ordinary language.
8. When you use a word, you must put quotation marks around it.
9. If the intension is more specific, then the extension is broader.
10. If the extension is more specific, then the intension is broader.

4.4.2 *Directions:* Arrange the following terms in order of increasing the broad denotation, that is, most concrete to most abstract.

1. Automobile, Ford, Transportation, Physical Object, F-150
2. Man-made object, Chaise, Furniture, Indoor Sitting
3. Clothing, Tops, Formal Wear, Wool Stitched, Single-breasted Dinner Jacket
4. Living Organism, Dolphin, Aquatic-animal, Mammal, Fins

*5. Professor, Peter Singer, Scholar, Human, Man

e. Definitions

1. A definition includes the meaning of a word—both connotation and denotation. A definition is an explicit usage of words that assigns meaning to another word. If we think of a word as a symbol denoting a thing, then a definition includes more symbols to explain the original symbol, hopefully in a more straightforward way. It is possible that the meaning of a word is done in a way that is not simple and only adds more confusion. That is where we derive the saying, "the circularity of a dictionary definition."

2. Lexical definitions are most commonly found in the dictionary. This is the way in which a word is already used and accepted in our language. A lexical definition helps us clarify ambiguity and avoid equivocation. Supplying a dictionary definition can resolve semantic disputes.

   Pantheism: the denial of God's personality and expresses a tendency to identify God with nature. In other words, God and nature are synonymous with one another. If you are confused about the meaning of the word "Pantheism" all that you need to do is look up the definition, and the issue will be resolved. Thus, lexical definitions are either true or false depending on the consistency with the established definition. Usage of a term can change over time though. The word "barbarian" used to mean any person that is not Greek or Roman. If you were not of Greek or Roman descent, then you were a barbarian. Our current usage of the term is quite different. We use the word "barbarian" to refer to uncivilized savages of sorts. Just recently the word "they" may be used as a singular gender neutral pronoun.

3. Persuasive definitions are meant to elicit a positive or negative attitude toward the term being defined. A persuasive definition places a façade over the real meaning and passes the façade off as the actual meaning. This is usually done to condemn or praise the term based upon its definition. For example, a pro-life advocate might attempt to define abortion by using the word "murder" and in doing so have defined "abortion" in such a way that it is automatically considered wrong. "Murder" is by definition, the unjustified killing of innocent life. So, a pro-life advocate will assign that meaning to the term "abortion" to condemn that behavior.

   On the other hand, a pro-choice advocate will define the word "abortion" with the woman's autonomy over reproductive rights. The pro-choice advocate will use the word "abortion" as a means to preserve rights over choices with their body. Both instances show us something troubling about persuasive definitions, that is, the definition resolves the issue surrounding them rather than relying on moral arguments. Since these definitions are used to evoke positive or negative attitudes, the definitions cannot be classified as true or false.

4. Stipulative definitions coin a new word for the first time or add new meaning to an old word. Most slang words are stipulated, and most of which are old words and are being used in a new way. The phrase, "Netflix and chill" has a particular sort of meaning beyond what is ordinarily understood by those terms. This phrase has been stipulated both for use in slang and also to masquerade the proper meaning from those who should not be aware.

   During times of war, many terms were stipulated in order to pass orders over the radio waves, without the enemy listening in on it. For example, "The eagle has landed" is a ubiquitous descriptive phrase that could denote a significant figure reaching a particular destination that again is not explicitly disclosed. Since these are arbitrary assignments of meaning, these definitions cannot be classified as true or false. Hence, this is another reason why vagueness cannot be resolved by supplying *ad hoc* stipulative definitions to terms.

Exercise 4.5

4.5.1 *Directions:* Determine whether the following definitions are stipulative, persuasive, or lexical.

1. "Dowry" means a gift of money that a woman presents to a man at their marriage.
2. "Spife" means a spoon and a knife that is used to cut through and scoop the contents of a brownie sundae.
3. "Treadmill" means the endless and dreadful death march to nowhere.
4. "Brangelina" means the established power couple of Brad Pitt and Angelina Jolie.
5. "Aporia" means the point in which the evidence is equally justifying opposing sides.
6. "Religious Freedom" means discriminating against people who do not believe the same things that you do.
7. "Smorkle" means eating s'mores right before you go snorkeling.
8. "Besmear" means to defile or degrade to a lesser degree.
9. "Feminism" means the superiority of women above men, which includes reverse discrimination.

*10. "Precisify" means to make a term more precise than it currently is.

4.5.2 *Directions:* Determine whether the following statements are true or false.

1. Stipulative definitions are well accepted in our language and hence are either true or false.
2. Persuasive definitions are exactly what you would find in a dictionary.
3. The word "definition" does not have a definition.
4. Lexical definitions may change over time.
5. A definition is always an arbitrary assignment of meaning.

f. Informal Fallacies

Formal and Informal Fallacies:

A fallacy is a mistake in reasoning. Usually there is some sort of error from the premises to the conclusion. Fallacies have a surface plausibility, meaning that they appear to make arguments stronger than they actually are. Thus, it requires some training to spot fallacious reasoning. So, studying fallacies is helpful for a variety of reasons. Two reasons that are particularly important here are practical and theoretical. Practical reasons for studying fallacies involve learning about fallacies to make you a more effective arguer. Thus, in formal debates you will be able to spot poor reasoning, call it out for what it is, and offer counter-arguments. The theoretical reason is the same as what was stated at the beginning of this text. We study poor reasoning to hopefully provide us with some insight about good reasoning. Although you might be inclined to think that we should only study good reasoning and not waste your time on poor reasoning, this view is short-sighted. We are not able to understand good reasoning unless we are able to understand poor reasoning and why it fails. So, after a thorough study of fallacies, you'll be able to argue effectively and learn about good reasoning.

A formal fallacy involves evaluating the structure of an argument. A formal fallacy occurs in deductive arguments and occur independent of the content of an argument. We will discuss formal fallacies in the later section of this book. An informal fallacy is not an issue with structure, it is a problem with the content of an argument. Thus, they can be a bit more difficult to spot. All informal fallacies are found in weak inductive arguments. In an earlier section, we discussed a set of inductive arguments in which the conclusion follows with a high degree of probability. However, informal fallacies occur in weak arguments in which the conclusion follows with a low degree of probability. That is not to say, all weak inductive arguments are fallacious, but that all fallacious arguments are weak.[8] So, your ability to discern the strength of inductive arguments will be crucial in deciphering informal fallacies.

I have divided informal fallacies into three classes. Think of each class as a genus and the particular fallacies under that genus are a species. The three classes of fallacies are (1) *Fallacies Involving a Person*, (2) *Fallacies of Irrelevance*, and (3) *Fallacies of Methodical Approach*.

1. *Fallacies Involving a Person*

Fallacies in this category include arguments that have to do with a person or persons. They are attacking character, appealing to individual weaknesses, relying on expertise, imposing coercion, or tricking people.

---

[8] You may argue that all weak arguments are, in fact, fallacious. If we are ignorant of each and every informal fallacy, it is certainly possible that there is an unknown fallacy occurring in all weak arguments. However, this concern is outside the scope of this textbook.

(1) *Argumentum ad Populum* (Appeal to the People)

This type of fallacy involves the element of camaraderie, which is the idea that there is a shared experience among a group of people. Mainly, we like to be part of a larger group. When we surround ourselves with like-minded people, we have a sense of belonging. So, this fallacy uses that element to make people believe their argument. This includes many different variations: mob mentality, fear mongering, bandwagon, vanity, snobbery, and tradition.

Mob mentality does exactly what the name suggests, it appeals to mobs of people who are likely to be more complacent. Whenever there is a social injustice, people usually take to the streets for a protest. As the mob gets more and more angry, things tend to escalate very quickly. So, what begins as a demonstration quickly becomes a destructive force. Someone will eventually yell, "Let's Riot!" and suddenly people, whom would never otherwise be involved, find themselves part of this destructive force. This is also found at comedy shows. The opening act is meant to loosen up the audience and get them laughing. I am sure that most of you have been with a group of friends whom are laughing and it in turn makes you laugh even more.

There is another type of appeal to the people that is relying on a brute emotion, that is, *fear*. Fear mongering is when you spread fear among a large group of people to scare them so much that they are willing to alter their lives. The George Orwell novel "1984" is an easy illustration of that.[9] Big brother is watching you and thus you are going to change your life accordingly. Adolf Hitler was able to convince an entire nation to take up arms. He blamed the Jewish population for subversive elements of the state, and that if nothing was done about it, you would lose everything.

We are all very familiar with the bandwagon argument. It goes something like, "All of my friends are going bridge jumping in Ann Arbor, so I want to go as well." So, because other people are doing it, then I should do it as well. This, as explained by your parents, is very odd. Just because there are a bunch of other people who have murdered people does not justify you murdering people. Nor does it deny any responsibility for what you have done. Stating in court that other people murder will not remove your responsibility for acting as such.

As a child you probably watched superheroes and thought that if you did what they were doing, then you might have a shot at being them. Thus, Popeye would always eat an entire can of spinach in order for his muscles to grow exponentially. So, vanity is when you do something because some famous figure did it. Most celebrity endorsements rely on an appeal to vanity. As soon as the celebrity begins to endorse the product, sales increase substantially.

[9] Orwell, George. *1984.* London: Secker and Warburg, 1949. Print.

An appeal to vanity is meant to get everyone on board, but snobbery is only meant to get a subset of the population on board. This is when you appeal to only a small elite group of individuals. Thus, country clubs will have signs that are accepting applications for those with considerable means. That is, we want to recruit people, but only very wealthy people.

The final version is appeal to tradition. We have always done it that way, so we should continue to do it that way. People have been doing this for centuries, so notwithstanding it being morally impermissible, we should keep doing it. There have been plenty of practices that were traditions, but the fact that they were traditions does not necessarily mean that we should keep doing them. Human sacrifices were common in many areas of the world. Just because they were a tradition though, does not mean we should continue performing human sacrifices.

(2) *Ad Hominem* (Attack the Person)

An ad hominem occurs when you attack the person rather than their argument. This occurs when the person is either incapable or unwilling to address the central claims of their opponent's argument. Thus, an opponent decides to attack the person's character, and then dismiss the argument on those grounds. *Ad hominem* involves four different types: abusive, circumstantial, tu quoque, and poisoning the well.

An abusive *ad hominem* involves verbal attacks on a person. So, when you attack their character instead of their claims, you have committed an abusive ad hominem. So, it occurs when someone argues in favor of progressive taxes, and then an opponent says "John is a lazy, pathetic, idiot who has no idea what they are talking about."

A circumstantial *ad hominem* involves alluding to the circumstances that the arguer is part of, and then says that is the only reason why they are arguing as such. So, because you are benefitting from arguing that way, that is the only reason you argue that way. For example, "You argue for increases to welfare because you receive welfare. If you did not receive welfare, then you would not argue that way."

The tu quoque *ad hominem* is oftentimes referred to as the "You too" fallacy. It occurs when you claim that the arguer is being hypocritical because in other aspects of their life, they do something quite similar. "You cannot condemn certain behaviors because you do those kinds of behaviors." However, whether or not you engage in such activities is irrelevant when determining if the action is permissible or not. Your parents probably told you to not party in high school. Telling your parents that you will party anyways because they used to party in high school does not address the crux of the problem.

The last *ad hominem* variation involves poisoning the well. This occurs when the opponent dismisses your argument before you have had a chance to present your argument. It is stopping the process before it even begins. A common example of this is mansplaining. This occurs when a man cuts off a woman before she has a chance to speak, and condescendingly tries to explain it directly to them.

(3) *Argumentum ad Misericordiam* (Appeal to Pity)

This fallacy occurs when you attempt to evoke emotion from the listener to get them to accept your conclusion. You do not have logical grounds to support your conclusion, so you rely on emotive rhetoric instead. For example, "If we cut the educational funding, then poor and helpless little children will suffer and not be able to get a job." These fallacies occur when rhetoric replaces the logic.

(4) *Argumentum ad Baculum* (Appeal to Force)

This involves threatening you either physically or psychologically to get you to accept their conclusion. So, in other words, you will receive some harm if you do not accept this conclusion. You might be inclined to think, out of self-preservation, that it is a good reason to just accept the conclusion. However, this is not a good logical reason to accept it. The former shows why this fallacy is so often used because of its effectiveness. For example, "Either you give me your candy or I'm telling mom that you broke her vase." This is an example of psychological harm that will come. You are blackmailing the other child. A physical threat might be, "The Walking Dead is the best show on television, and if you deny it, then my friend will beat you over the head with a baseball bat wrapped in barbed wire."

(5) *Argumentum ad Verecundiam* (Appeal to Unqualified Authority)

Arguments based upon an authority are such that the conclusion depends on a claim made by a professed expert. However, with the appeal to unqualified authority, you are drawing a conclusion based upon an expert, who is not really an expert in that field. For example, "My Sociology professor argues that morality is entirely relative to different cultures. Since they study different cultures, they are correct about moral relativism."

(6) Straw Man

The straw man fallacy occurs when an arguer presents a particular position, and the opponent sets up a different argument from the original, demolishes the altered argument, and then claims to have beaten the original argument. So, the person sets up a straw man of their opponent and only attacks the fake version rather than the original argument. For example, "Wakefield argues that we should protect the freedom of speech to all citizens notwithstanding the groups they are affiliated with. But that means that we should endorse neo-Nazi hate speech. But that kind of hate speech incites riots and violence to helpless citizens. Obviously, Wakefield has no idea what he is talking about."

(7) Red Herring

This fallacy is very closely related to the straw man fallacy. This fallacy is more subtle than the straw man. The straw man sets up a new argument and makes an explicit attack against it. Thus, hoping to dismiss the original argument as well. However, the red herring is when you subtly change the topic in the middle of the argument without the listener noticing. The red herring does not include the knock down at the end like the straw man does. For example, "Violent video games are corrupting the youth of this country and we should impose some kind of censorship on the video games. But there are some video games that are very realistic. Grand Theft Auto V is such an elaborate and interesting game. You can switch between different characters without going back the main menu. This game is revolutionary."

Exercise 4.6

4.6.1 *Directions:* Identify the correct fallacy being committed in the following arguments. Select the fallacy from the list of *Fallacies Involving a Person.*

1. The practice of infanticide is completely immoral. However, people kill other people during times of war. It is also the case that we are justified in going to war. War is sometimes justified for the preservation of humanity.

2. Jenny McCarthy argues that vaccinations cause autism and other health-related issues. Since Jenny McCarthy is a well-respected celebrity and well versed in public concerns, we should believe what she says.

*3. You often vote Republican in elections. But you are a business owner, and you will see the immediate benefits of the tax-cuts. Clearly, the only reason that you vote Republican is because you will directly benefit from voting that way.

4. In the United States, people are so unwilling to endorse universal healthcare to all citizens. But look at other countries. Austria, Denmark, Finland, and Sweden are all countries that have universal healthcare. We should follow their lead.

5. Ben Shapiro argues against abortion in all cases and that the government should make legislation forbidding the practice. But Shapiro argues in favor of a state religion. A state religion leads to the oppression of the citizens. People will be persecuted for believing in a religion outside of what the state has adopted. This is what happens with Authoritarian governments. Is that what we want for the United States? I don't think so. Ben Shapiro's arguments should be dismissed.

6. "We must rid the world of evil, now is the time to draw a line in the sand against the evil ones, across the world and across the years, we will fight the evil ones, and we will win, you are either for us or against us!"[10]

7. We have provided you with the protective services that you asked for. Now, you want to avoid paying for this service. I don't care if you have no money, your family is hungry, and business is slow. Pay me! If you don't get me the money right now, then you'll be sleeping with the fishes.

8. We should applaud those individuals whom are responsible for all of the job creation in this country. The top 1% are often criticized for being the villains. However, these people made this country and deserve to be praised.

9. I know that I was caught cheating on the midterm professor. But if you fail me in this class, then I will not get into the nursing program. Nursing is very important to me. Many sick people in this world need my help and will die if I don't assist them. Surely, you will not fail me in this course.

---

[10] Bush, George W. *State of the Union Address. https://georgewbush-whitehouse.archives.gov/news/releases/2002/01/20020129-11.html*

10. In the past few weeks, there have been outbreaks of Ebola in this country. Hospitals are preparing special wings to deal with these outbreaks. You should be careful where you go and who you talk to. Make sure that people you are around have not been to Africa in the past year. It's probably best to stay in your homes until these outbreaks have been eradicated.

11. You argue that we should decrease the amount of CO_2 emissions and that the United Nations should take steps to reduce the green houses gases being contributed by all countries. However, you flew to the U.N. conference on a private jet. Obviously, your arguments against CO_2 emissions are nonsense.

12. Kendall Jenner posted on her Instagram account that she struggled her entire life with bad skin complexity. Thus, after trying many different products, she realized that Proactiv was the only product that shows results. Since she has millions of followers, she clearly knows what she's talking about.

13. You are never willing to show me that you appreciate me. Last week, when we were at the mall, I saw those beautiful diamond earrings. If you want to stay with me, then you should consider getting me those earrings.

14. John Oliver argues that bullying is running rampant in this country. But Oliver is not even from this country. He is a loud, pretentious, liberal pundit. He is not the respectful reporter that people think he is.

15. Every year my family eats Paczkis on fat Tuesday. Therefore, we should continue to eat them each and every year.

4.6.2 *Directions:* Please describe some of the differences between the following fallacies. Write a few sentences explaining the difference. Please answer in your own words.

1. *Straw Man* and *Red Herring*
2. *Appeal to Force* and *Appeal to Pity*
3. *Ad Hominem* abusive and *Ad Hominem* circumstantial

2. *Fallacies of Irrelevance*

Fallacies in this category include arguments that lack a strong connection between the premises and the conclusion. However, these arguments are purporting to have a strong connection. So, in other words, the premises are completely irrelevant to the conclusion.

(1) Hasty Generalization

When we discussed the inductive forms in an earlier section, we covered a generalization. A generalization is when you select a small sample from a larger group, and then characterize the entire group based upon the small sample. However, the hasty generalization is a weak version of that argument. The hasty generalization occurs when the small sample does not represent the entire group. So, the small sample usually includes outliers of the larger group. So, you cannot generalize the entire group from a few outliers. For example, "Five people in Michigan said that they voted for Hilary Clinton because she is a female notwithstanding her policies. So, it is quite clear that policies did not matter for anyone who voted for her."

(2) Slippery Slope

A slippery slope is a type of reasoning that begins with a plausible first step, but once you take the first step, you slide all the way to the bottom. In an argument, you begin with a plausible premise, but once you grant that, then the argument follows a chain reaction whereas the conclusion does not follow at all from the first premise. For example, "If we allow same-sex marriage, then what's to stop people from marrying their siblings or cousins? But, if we allow people to marry their siblings or cousins, then what's to stop them from marrying their pets? If we allow people to marry their pets, then what's to stop them from marrying a horse? If people marry a horse, then they will marry inanimate objects. But, if people marry a toaster, then there will be no procreation. The end of procreation is the end of humanity."

(3) False Dichotomy

The false dichotomy occurs with disjunctive syllogisms. You are probably thinking, this form is deductive and hence does not belong in the section on informal fallacies. In part, that is correct. Nonetheless, this fallacy does not occur in the form itself, rather the fallacy occurs in the content of the argument. A dichotomy is a set of options, specifically two. In order for the disjunctive syllogism to be valid, the set of options must be mutually exclusive and jointly exhaustive. So, the two options must exhaust all of the possibilities. If there are more than just two possibilities, then the argument is committing the false dichotomy. So, essentially the fallacy occurs when you present two options, deny one of them, and then assert the other option. But, if there are more than just two options, then it does not follow that the denial of one allows you to infer the other option. For example, "Let me go see Lady Gaga or I will die. You don't want me to die. So, you should let me go see Lady Gaga."

(4) *Ignoratio Elenchi* (Missing the Point)

This fallacy occurs when the premises support one conclusion, but a different conclusion is being drawn. You often hear the phrase, "Jumping to conclusions." So, think of this fallacy involving people who jump to conclusions. Usually a person will assume more than what is contained in the premises. For example, "People abuse alcohol on a regular basis. The only option is to prohibit the use of alcohol altogether."

(5) *Argumentum ad Ignorantiam* (Appeal to Ignorance)

This fallacy may be confused with the previous fallacy. The previous fallacy occurs when you make a leap from what the premises imply to a wrong conclusion. The appeal to ignorance fallacy occurs when the premises admit that one thing has not been proven, and then makes a definite assertion from that ignorance. For example, "People have been trying to prove the existence of miracles for thousands of years. Nobody has been successful in their pursuits. Therefore, we should conclude that miracles are patently false."

(6) False Cause

False cause fallacies occur when the link between the cause and the anticipated effect or the effect and the anticipated cause is not strong enough. You might be familiar with the phrase, "Correlation does not equal causation." This means that just because two things are correlates of one another, does not mean that one of those things is the cause of the other. We base causation on past experience. You have no special insight into the nature of causation itself. When you see one event followed by another event, and this pattern repeats itself over and over, you eventually impose causation onto those two events. The false cause occurs when you don't have the extensive amount of experience of those things happening in the past to justify that type of inference in the future. The false cause fallacy has three variations: *post hoc ergo propter hoc*, oversimplified cause, and gambler's fallacy.

The *post hoc ergo propter hoc* (after this, therefore, because of this) is a version of the fallacy that relies on temporal succession. One event happens and then another event happens and you think that there is a causal connection. Most superstitions are based on the *post hoc*. For example, "Every time Tiger Woods wins a golf tournament, he wears a red shirt on the final day. Therefore, in the future each time he wears a red shirt he will likely win the tournament."

The oversimplified cause occurs when you take a complex and dynamic situation and reduce it down to one simple cause. In doing so, you dismiss all of the other causes that are bringing about the effect. For example, "Traffic is absolutely horrible right now. We have not moved in nearly twenty minutes. Obviously, some incompetent driver is the reason for this."

The gambler's fallacy was coined in the middle ages based upon a type of reasoning that has to do with gambling itself. This reasoning occurs with people who are not familiar with probability theory. You might think that probability contains an element of causation. However, probability includes independent events. Suppose that I were to flip a fair-sided coin ten times in a row. The probability is that 5/10 flips will be heads. So, people would reason in such a way that if a person flipped the coin five times in a row and got heads that the next flip has to be tails. So, people in the middle ages would bet their entire life savings on the flip landing on tails, only to find out that the flip turned out to be heads. Each flip carries a 50/50 chance of being heads or tails. Flip number 2 and flip number 4 have nothing to do with flip number 3. Each flip is an independent event; so, the fallacy occurs when you think that there is a causal link between independent events.

Exercise 4.6 continued

4.6.3 *Directions:* Identify the correct fallacy being committed in the following arguments. Select the fallacy from the list of *Fallacies of Irrelevance.*

*1. I used to work for the Federal government. The government does a really good job convincing the people that things are one way, when in fact, things are entirely different. You cannot trust the government at all. Thus, you should not dismiss conspiracy theories as crack-pot theories because they are all true.

2. Each time that I forget to wear my wristwatch to work, I get stuck at every single traffic light. So, I should make sure that if I don't want to sit at every light, then I need to wear my wristwatch.

3. Steve argues in favor of increases to social programs. But if we increase social programs, then people will exploit the system. Once people exploit the system, they will no longer have an incentive to work. Once people lose the incentive to work, they will become socialists. Socialism leads to communism where the workers own all means of production. And communist nations lead to the destruction of innovation.

4. The Argument Clinic, Macomb's premiere philosophy club, has had four female presidents. Thus, only females are fit for officer positions.

5. There is no evidence that shows marijuana is detrimental to your health. It follows that anti-marijuana ads are mistaken, and marijuana is not harmful.

6. According to the SEC, securities fraud has increased substantially over the past decade. Obviously, online trading is the sole reason for this.

7. The professor does not recall assigning the homework from section 4.6. It follows from this that the professor is suffering from amnesia.

8. I was digging post holes in my backyard to install a fence. After digging down about 6 inches, I hit solid clay that made in nearly impossible to dig through. So, the entire backyard has solid clay under the soil.

9. After entering the party store and purchasing a few scratch off lottery tickets, I was frustrated that they were losers. So, if I go back into the store and buy a few more, I am guaranteed to get a winner. After all, the odds of winning are 1: 3.75.

10. It is nearly impossible to determine when life begins. So, to make things easier, life begins at conception.

4.6.4 *Directions:* Please describe some of the differences between the following fallacies. Write a few sentences explaining the difference. Please answer in your own words.

1. *Post Hoc Ergo Propter Hoc* and *Slippery Slope*
2. *Missing the Point* and *Appeal to Ignorance*

3. *Fallacies of Methodical Approach*

Fallacies in this category include arguments that make a mistake in the process of reasoning from the premises to the conclusion. This error occurs when you reason from content in the premises to mistaken content in the conclusion. That is not to say there is an issue in the structure though.

(1) *Petitio Principii* (Begging the Question)

Begging the question is a type of reasoning whereas you use a premise to prove the exact same claim in the conclusion. This fallacy involves reasoning in a circle. You are assuming the very thing that you are trying to prove. This fallacy has three variations: leaving out a contentious premise, synonymous language, and arguing in a circle. The first type is when you omit a certain premise because that premise is contentious and may be debated. Rather than including the premise, you omit the premise in hopes that the listener does not recognize that it is missing and they are more likely to accept the conclusion. For example, "Things that are unnatural are immoral, so it follows that same-sex marriage immoral." This is begging the question because you should ask, "Is same-sex marriage unnatural?" In other words, the argument assumes that same-sex marriage is unnatural to then say that it is, in fact, immoral.

The second variation is using synonymous language. This occurs when you use a term or set of terms in the premises that are synonymous to a term or set of terms used in the conclusion. In this sense, you are essentially restating the very same claim you made in the premises. An example of this occurs in the *Euthyphro* dialogue written by Plato.[11] Socrates was inquiring about the nature of "piety" to prepare for his upcoming trial. Euthyphro, the expert on religion in Athens, states that "God's commands are right." Socrates then inquires whether actions are right because God commands them or if they are right and that is why God commands them? For Euthyphro to respond that actions are right and that is why God commands them would make both himself and the Gods mere messengers. Euthyphro responds that actions are right because God commands them. If all actions that God commands are right, and all right actions are commanded by God, then this implies and unsavory conclusion. That is because "God's commands" and "Right" are being used synonymously. So, it is possible to replace "God's commands" with "Right" and retain the same meaning. So, Socrates notices that it is possible to take the statement "God's commands are right" and replace that with "God's commands are God's commands," which is an empty truism. Thus, Euthyphro is begging the question.

The third variation is when you reason in a circle. This occurs when you are assuming the very same thing that you are trying to prove. In this variation of the fallacy, you do not know where the argument begins or ends. For example, "Of course God exists. God wrote the bible, and it says in the bible that God exists." You are assuming that he exists to then write the bible, and then using that assumption as evidence that he does, in fact, exist.

---

[11] Plato. *Five Dialogues : Euthyphro, Apology, Crito, Meno, Phaedo.* Indianapolis: Hackett Pub. Co., 2002. Print.

(2) Equivocation

This fallacy involves either a term or a phrase that is being used ambiguously in the premises to derive a conclusion using the same term or phrase in a different sense. In other words, the definition of the term or phrase is not being consistently used throughout the argument. For example, "Nothing is better than happiness. A peanut butter and jelly sandwich is better than nothing. Therefore, a peanut butter and jelly sandwich is better than happiness." The word "nothing" is being used in two different senses. The first usage is referring to no single thing is better than happiness. The second usage is referring to pure *nothingness.* We would not all agree that there is no single thing that is better than a peanut butter and jelly sandwich. In fact, many things are better than a peanut butter and jelly sandwich. So, this sense of "nothing" is pure *nothingness*. So, *something* is better than *nothing*.

(3) Composition

This fallacy occurs when you assume that because all of the parts of a whole contain a certain property that the whole contains that very same property. You are attempting to transfer a property from the parts to the same property in the whole. For example, "Every member of President Trump's cabinet has feet, therefore, President Trump's cabinet has feet." The cabinet is an abstract class of constituents. So, even though all of the referents have feet, it does not follow that the abstract class has feet.

(4) Division

This fallacy is the complete opposite of the fallacy of composition. This occurs when you assume that because the whole contains a certain property that the parts of the whole contain the very same property. You are attempting to transfer a property from the whole to the same property in the parts. For example, "This Ford F-150 is made in America, therefore, all of the parts are made in America." We assemble the vehicle in America, but it does not follow that we made all of the parts in America. We usually get the parts from overseas, and then assemble those parts together in America.

(5) Weak Analogy

An analogy is when you say that two different things are similar to one another such that certain characteristics you find in one thing are more than likely to be found in the similar thing as well. A weak analogy is when you compare two similar things and try to extrapolate characteristics from the one to the other, when in fact, the two things being compared are not similar enough to do that. For example, "Before you buy a new pair of shoes, you should walk around in them and make sure that they serve you well. Similarly, before you marry someone you should take them for a test run to make sure they serve you well." This is a weak analogy because shoes are an ordinary commodity. You use the shoes as an instrument to get around. When the shoes no longer serve you well, you throw them away and get a new pair. A human being is intrinsically valuable and not merely instrumentally valuable. Thus, humans deserve to be treated with dignity and respect. So, you do not marry a person to use them as if they were a tool and then when the tool no longer serves you, you then throw them into the garbage and get a new one.

Exercise 4.6 continued

4.6.5 *Directions:* Identify the correct fallacy being committed in the following arguments. Select the fallacy from the list of *Fallacies of Methodical Approach.*

1. Everything that runs has feet. Rivers run. Therefore, rivers have feet.
2. The American Philosophical Association is 114 years old. Therefore, each and every member of the American Philosophical Association is 114 years old.
3. Professional athletes practice at least ten hours per day during the season, and half of that during the off-season. Therefore, students in introduction to logic should be studying ten hours per day during the semester, and half that during all other times.
4. Every player on the team is exceptional. Therefore, the team itself is exceptional.
5. I encounter decisions each and every day. I have made many choices in the past, all of which were from my own volition. Therefore, I am free to make choices and determinism is false.

*6. Millennials are so soft nowadays. Make sure to not let them fall down.

7. I made a painting in my art class at Macomb Community College. So, it follows that the paint was made in my art class at Macomb Community College.
8. Two-wheeled modes of transportation are all the same. Since I am very familiar with riding a single speed bicycle, I will have no problem riding the Honda 750 motorcycle that I just got.
9. All of the parts of the board game are blue-colored. So, the board game is blue-colored.
10. My best friend is obsequious because they are dutiful and overly obedient when needed.

4.6.6 *Directions:* Please describe some of the differences between the following fallacies. Write a few sentences explaining the difference. Please answer in your own words.

1. *Composition* and *Division*
2. *Weak Analogy* and *Equivocation*
3. The three variations of *Begging the Question*

SECTION V

Formal Logic

a. Syllogistic logic

1. Categorical Propositions

Propositions relate two classes or domains, that is, categories. More specifically, a proposition is a relation between a subject and a predicate. The predicate qualifies over the subject. Propositions are true, if and only if, there is a state of affairs such that the subject at T_1 has a particular predicate at T_1. Respectively, the subject of a proposition is called the *subject term*, and the predicate of the proposition is called the *predicate term*. In this section, propositions are classified into four different possibilities. Either all or part of the subject class is included in or excluded from the predicate class. Standard-form categorical propositions must be one of the following types, which is clear, unambiguous, and exhaustive.

A, E, I, O

A: All S are P

Every member of the subject class is included in the predicate class.

E: No S are P

Every member of the subject class is excluded from the predicate class.

I: Some S are P

At least one member of the subject class is included in the predicate class.

O: Some S are not P

At least one member of the subject class is excluded from the predicate class.

Quantifiers

A quantifier is the first word of a standard-form proposition, which includes, "All," "No," and "Some". They specify how much of the subject class is included in or excluded from the predicate class. "All" must include every member of the subject class, such that every member of the subject class is included in the predicate class. "No" means that there are no members of the subject class that are included in the predicate class. "Some" has a particular meaning in logic. "Some" means that there is at least one member of the subject class that is included in or excluded from the predicate class. "Some" could mean more than one or possibly "All," but those are merely speculative without content. For it is the content of the subject term and predicate term that dictates the specific amount of the word "Some." For our purposes, we will restrict "Some" to mean at least one.

Another important note in the logic is that "Some S are P" does not imply that "Some S are not P" and "Some S are not P" does not imply that "Some S are P." Although we may think it is natural to infer the one from the other, it is not permissible in logic. We are focused primarily on form and structure. There is nothing about the form of "Some S are P" that implies "Some S are not P." There will be some examples that allow that inference, but others that will not. For example, since "Some" may imply "All," we may say that if it does, then "Some S are not P" is false, but if it does not, then "Some S are not P" is true. So, "Some restaurants are fast food establishments" does not imply that "All restaurants are fast food establishments." So, in this case, "Some restaurants are not fast food establishments" is true. However, "Some cats are animals" does imply that "All cats are animals," and the proposition, "Some cats are not animals" is false. Strictly speaking, the form alone does not allow for any inferences between the "I" and "O" propositions.

Quality/Quantity

When we use the word "quality" we are positively or negatively regarding something in particular. Think about purchasing "high-quality" items. An item is considered "high quality" if and only if it is regarded in the most positive way. In Logic, we use quality to refer to an affirmative or negative relationship. That is, the quality of a proposition is affirmative when there is a positive relationship between the subject and the predicate. The quality of a proposition is negative when there is a negative relationship between the subject and the predicate. So, you should consider if the relationship is affirmed or denied between the subject term and the predicate term.

All S are P—Affirmative

No S are P—Negative

Some S are P—Affirmative

Some S are not P—Negative

The propositions "A," and "I" are both affirmative. They are expressing a positive relationship between the subject term and the predicate term. On the other hand, "E," and "O" are both negative. They are expressing a negative relationship between the subject term and the predicate term.

When we use the word "quantity" we are referring to the way in which we might classify each of the four standard-form categorical propositions. This is not to be confused with quantifiers. Quantifiers are terms denoting the amount of each subject class, whereas quantity is classifying whole propositions. Thus, propositions are either *universal* or *existential*. A proposition is said to be universal if it is true in every possible situation. So, "A" and "E" are universal because they are general claims that are true in every situation. A proposition is said to be existential if it is true in certain situations, but not all. Thus, "I" and "O" are existential because they refer to a small class that is only true part of the time.

All S are P—Universal

No S are P—Universal

Some S are P—Existential

Some S are not P—Existential

Copula

A *copula* is a linking verb in ordinary English. This may include but is not limited to: "are," "are not," "is," "is not," "were," and "were not." The copula connects the subject and the predicate. In other words, the copula signifies the relationship between the subject and the predicate. Look at the following example below:

All members of the American Philosophical Association are people holding advanced degrees from accredited academic institutions.

Quantifier:	All
Subject term:	members of the American Philosophical Association
Copula:	are
Predicate term:	people holding advanced degrees from accredited academic institutions.

Distribution

A term is distributed if and only if the proposition makes an assertion about every member of the class; otherwise it's undistributed. So, if the proposition makes an assertion about every member of the *P* class, then *P* is distributed. If it makes an assertion about every member of the *S* class, then *S* is distributed; otherwise *S* and *P* are undistributed. So, you should determine whether the proposition is referring to the entirety of the class being denoted.

	Distribution
All S are P	S
No S are P	S and P
Some S are P	None
Some S are not P	P

Venn Diagrams

John Venn was a nineteenth-century logician and philosopher who created Venn diagrams. Venn diagrams are a visual aid to show the relation between the two classes. Venn diagrams are used in logic, set theory, and probability theory. Thus, there are four different Venn diagrams for each of the four standard-form categorical propositions.

For brevity's sake, we should name each section of the Venn diagram in order to refer to those areas.

Figures created by Bradley Wakefield.

When filling in the Venn diagrams, you should follow these two steps: (1) shade the negative space for all universals and (2) mark an "X" for all existentials. Shading in logic is different from shading in math. In math, shading represents that there is something inside of the shaded area. In logic, shading means emptiness. So, when you shade an area, you are expressing an empty area. We denote an "X" for existentials. Existential statements are referring to an *S* that either is or is not a *P*. So, we mark the one *S* with an "X." The diagrams for the four categorical propositions are as follows:

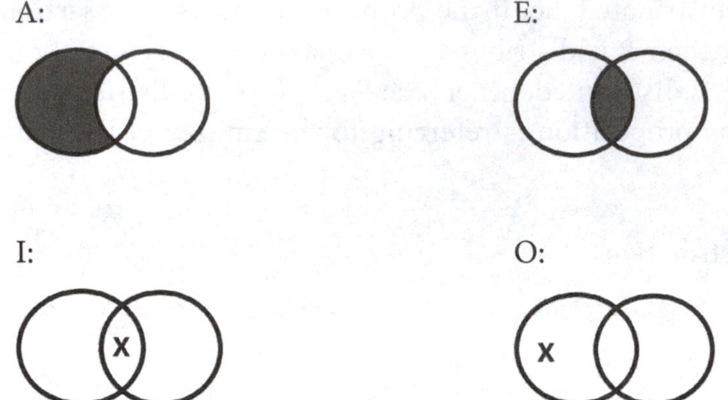

Figures created by Bradley Wakefield.

Exercise 5.1

5.1.1 *Directions:* For each of the following propositions identify the letter name, quality, quantity, and whether the subject term and predicate term are distributed.

1. All graduate students are people who have taken the GRE, LSAT, MCAT, or GMAT entrance exams.
2. Some politicians are beholden to their donors.
3. No skiers are snowboarders.
4. Some professors are not pompous individuals.
5. Some civil rights activists are humanitarians.
6. All swimming pools are filled with chemicals.
7. No countries are continents.
8. Some basketball players are not croquet players.

5.1.2 *Directions:* Change the quantity without changing the quality of the following statements:

*1. No Bernese mountain dogs are vicious animals.
2. All cats are creepy.
3. Some businesses are tax-exempt entities.
4. Some holidays are not globally recognized.

5.1.3 *Directions:* Change the quality without changing the quantity of the following statements:

*1. Some robots are not self-autonomous beings.
2. Some paintings are truly great works of art.
3. All barns are used as storage facilities.
4. No social media stars are celebrities.

5.1.4 *Directions:* Change both the quality and the quantity of the following statements:

*1. No books are newspapers.
2. Some philosophers are not economists.
3. Some handmade bespoke suits are carefully constructed pieces of art.
4. All fireplaces are warm additions to homes.

2. Existential Import

Existential Import: A statement has existential import if and only if the truth of the statement depends on the existence of a class contained in the statement, specifically, the subject class. Philosophers have agreed with one another that both of the existential statements (I and O) have existential import. Both of those propositions are speaking about the existence of the subject class. "I" means there exists one member of the subject class that is a member of the predicate class. "O" means there exists one member of the subject class is not a member of the predicate class. Both "I" and "O" are implying that there exists a member of the subject class. However, we cannot say the same about universals. One the one hand, "All cats are animals" seems to suggest that there are cats and that this class is also in a larger class of animals.

On the other hand, "All unicorns are majestic animals" seems to suggest that there are no unicorns that are also majestic animals. So, some will say that the former has existential import while the latter is lacking existential import. Do universals imply that the subject term has existential import? The issue over universals has been of great debate amongst philosophers. From this debate, two thinkers have provided positions on existential import. Aristotle is open to universals having existential import, while Boole is closed to universals having existential import.

Aristotle is open to universals having existential import insofar as the subject class being denoted actually exists. If the subject class actually exists, then the statement has existential import. If the subject class does not exist, then the statement does not have existential import. Thus, existential import is contingent upon the existence of the subject class being denoted.

Boole is closed to universals having existential import notwithstanding the existence of the subject class. Even if the subject class exists, it does not matter. Thus, existential import does not depend upon the existence of the subject class; it is merely closed in universals. Boole thinks that universals can still be true, but they must be understood as a conditional statement. "All cats are animals" is properly understood as "If it is a cat, then it is an animal." This universal proposition does not imply that there are cats or that they exist, but merely a relation between a sufficient condition and a necessary condition. "All centaurs are brave creatures" is properly understood as "If it is a centaur, then it is a brave creature." This universal proposition is merely expressing a hypothetical scenario between a sufficient condition and a necessary condition.

3. Square of Opposition

Modern and Traditional

(1a) Modern Square of Opposition

Since Boole has a narrow view that does not include as many valid inferences as Aristotle, we will begin with the Boolean system. Then, once we have a firm understanding of the modern square, we will move to the traditional square that Aristotle put forth.

A contradiction is a set of jointly exhaustive and mutually exclusive claims that cannot be simultaneously posited together without the complete annihilation of one or the other. Thus, the truth-value of one proposition necessitates the truth-value of the constituent part. So, for any proposition, *P* and its jointly exhaustive counterpart *Q*; if *P* is true, then *Q* is false. Conversely, if *Q* is true, then *P* is false. Upon a review of the four categorical propositions, we shall discover that there are two sets of jointly exhaustive and mutually exclusive propositions. "A" and "O" are contradictions of one another. "A" claims that "All S are P," meaning that every member of the subject class is included in the predicate class. "O" claims that "Some S are not P," meaning there is at least one member of the subject class that is excluded from the predicate class. These two propositions are expressing a direct contradiction of one another. It is impossible to be *all* and *not all* simultaneously without contradiction.

Similarly, "E" and "I" are contradictions of one another. "E" claims that "No S are P," meaning that there are no members of the subject class that are included in the predicate class. "I" claims that "Some S are P," meaning that there is at least one member of the subject class that is included in the predicate class. These two propositions are expressing a direct contradiction of one another. It is impossible to be *empty* and *not empty* simultaneously without contradiction. Thus, Boole has created the following modern square of opposition (see diagram below).

The next question to ask is, "What about the truth-values around the perimeter of the square?" Boole claims that these truth-values are undetermined. That is not to say that they do not have a truth-value, but that logic alone cannot provide you with the truth-value. The content of the subject term and predicate term determine the truth-value around the perimeter.

The Modern Square of Opposition

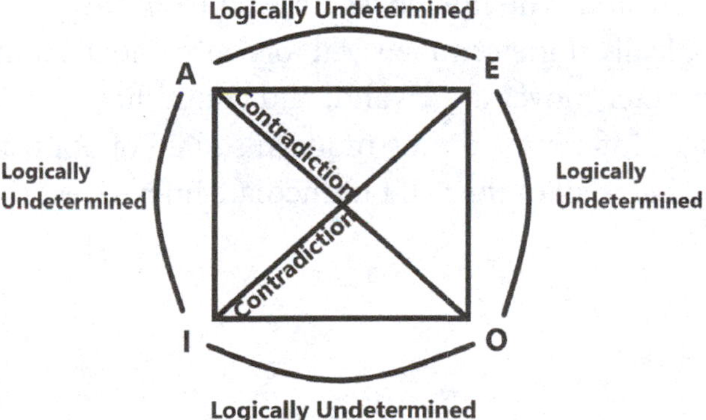

Figure created by Bradley Wakefield.

Testing Immediate Inferences using the Modern Square of Opposition

We always begin to test validity by assuming the premise is true. In light of that assumption, we test if there is an interpretation in which the premise is true, and the conclusion is false. If there is such an interpretation, then the argument is invalid. If there is no interpretation, then the argument is valid. We can use the modern square of opposition to test whether specific argument forms are valid. Look at the following example below:

All Bernese mountain dogs are friendly companions.

∴ Some Bernese mountain dogs are not friendly companions.

We first assume that the premise is true. In light of that assumption, is it possible for the conclusion to be false? In this particular argument, it is possible. So, we put a "T" next to the "A" on the modern square of opposition. Since the conclusion is an "O," we test the validity of the argument. If "A" is true, then by the contradictory relation "O" must be false. So, since the premise is a true "A" and the conclusion is a false "O," the argument has a true premise and a false conclusion, that is, it's invalid.

All Bernese mountain dogs are friendly companions.

∴ It is false that some Bernese mountain dogs are not friendly companions.

We first assume that the premise is true. In light of that assumption, it is possible for the conclusion to be false? We should put a "T" on the diagram next to the "A" on the modern square of opposition. The conclusion, "It is false that some Bernese mountain dogs are not friendly companions" is not in standard form. Standard-form categorical propositions must always begin with a quantifier. This conclusion does not begin with a quantifier. Since the conclusion *is false* and is stating that it *is false*, the conclusion is actually stating something that is true. When a proposition is preceded by "It is false that," then the proposition is the true contradictory statement. Thus, "It is false that some Bernese mountain dogs are not friendly companions" is not an "O" proposition, but rather, it is a true "A" proposition. So, the example above is an "A" premise and an "A" conclusion. So, the argument is valid.

If the immediate inference involves any sort of perimeter move on the modern square of opposition, it is invalid. The inferences derived from the perimeter of the modern square of opposition is logically undetermined. All logically undetermined inferences are invalid. That means that perimeter moves are invalid, and contradictory relations are invalid. This implies that the only valid inferences on the modern square of opposition are trivial arguments. The following list includes all of the valid immediate inferences:

(1) A

∴ A

(1) E

∴ E

(1) I

∴ I

(1) O

∴ O

Existential Fallacy: The existential fallacy is committed only when an argument is invalid merely because the premise lacks existential import. The existential fallacy occurs with a universal premise and an existential conclusion. However, A ∴ O, and E ∴ I are not existential fallacies. These two immediate inferences include a universal premise and an existential conclusion, but they are not invalid merely because the premise lacks existential import. They are invalid because they express a contradiction. A contradiction is of paramount significance. Thus, because the law of contradiction is the most important aspect of all of the classical logic, once it has been committed, it supersedes all other principles and fallacies. The existential fallacy may include but is not limited to:

All S are P. ∴ Some S are P.

No S are P. ∴ Some S are not P.

It is false that some S are not P. ∴ Some S are P.

It is false that some S are P. ∴ Some S are not P.

Exercise 5.2

5.2.1 *Directions:* Determine whether the following immediate inferences are valid or invalid using the modern square of opposition. Begin by assuming that the premise is true. Write "Existential Fallacy" if it occurs.

1. Some S are P. ∴ No S are P.
2. All S are P. ∴ Some S are not P.
3. No S are P. ∴ It is false that Some S are P.
4. Some S are not P. ∴ It is false that Some S are P.
5. It is false that No S are P. ∴ Some S are P.

*6. All S are P. ∴ Some S are P.

7. Some S are P. ∴ Some S are not P.
8. It is false that Some S are not P. ∴ All S are P.

5.2.2 *Directions:* Determine whether the following immediate inferences are valid or invalid using the modern square of opposition. Begin by assuming that the premise is true. Write "Existential Fallacy" if it occurs.

1. Some beetles are scary Coleopterans. Therefore, all beetles are scary Coleopterans.
2. No cats are animals that have nine lives. Therefore, it is false that some cats are animals that have nine lives.
3. All presidents are smooth-talking politicians. Therefore, it is false that some presidents are smooth-talking politicians.
4. It is false that some Greek gods are morally dubious beings. Therefore, some Greek gods are not morally dubious beings.

*5. Some skydivers are fearless human beings. Therefore, it is false that all skydivers are fearless human beings.

6. Some sports cars are not vehicles that most people can afford. Therefore, no sports car are vehicles that most people can afford.
7. It is false that all fairies are virtuous. Therefore, some fairies are not virtuous.
8. No wizards who cast spells are good-looking. Therefore, it is false that all wizards who cast spells are good-looking.

(1b) Traditional Square of Opposition

Now that we spent some time learning the Boolean square, we will shift our attention to the Aristotelian square. Aristotle is open to existence for universals if the subject class actually exists. Since he is allowing for more inferences, this is providing a broader scope of validity. Thus, it would be inappropriate to use the modern square of opposition. Aristotle uses the traditional square of opposition that allows for some perimeter moves. Both Aristotle and Boole agree that existential propositions imply existential import. They are also in agreeance about contradictions. The traditional square functions much like the modern square, except for the additional perimeter moves for the traditional square. Aristotle introduces three perimeter moves: *contrary, subcontrary,* and *subalternate.*

A *contrary* relation is a set of mutually exclusive but not jointly exhaustive propositions that cannot be simultaneously true. Thus, if one of the contraries is true, then the other one is false. However, if one of the contraries is false, then we cannot determine the other true-value. The *contrary* relation is a partial contradiction. Mainly, it necessitates in one direction. Since a *contrary* is not jointly exhaustive, there are other possibilities beyond the two propositions. For example, "All apples are red" and "No apples are red" are two *contrary* propositions. So, if the former is true, the latter must be false. If the former is false, then we cannot say that the latter is true. Just because it is false that "All apples are red," does not itself imply that "No apples are red." Since these two are not jointly exhaustive, there are more options than the two. It is certainly possible that both of those propositions are false, being that "Some apples are red" and "Some apples are not red" are both true propositions.

Illicit contrary involves performing a wrong inference from the *contrary* relation. The illicit contrary includes moving from a false universal to the truth-value of its contrary.

A *subcontrary* relation is a set of jointly exhaustive propositions that cannot be simultaneously false. Thus, if one of the subcontraries is false, then the other one is true. However, if one of the subcontraries is true, then we cannot determine the other truth-value.

The *subcontrary* relation also functions as a partial contradiction. Mainly, it necessitates in one direction. When it comes to the *subcontrary* relation, one of the existential propositions must necessarily be true no matter what. There is no interpretation in which both the subcontraries are false. If that were the case, then we would have to say that there is also an interpretation in which two contraries are true (by the contradictory relation of both existentials being false). Since neither one of these interpretations is possible, the *contrary* and *subcontrary* relations function in direct opposition of one another.

Illicit subcontrary involves performing a wrong inference on the *subcontrary* relation. An illicit subcontrary includes moving from a true existential to the truth-value of its subcontrary.

A *subalternate* relation is a set of propositions that are not jointly exhaustive. This relation allows the truth to flow from certain propositions or for the falsity to flow from certain propositions. In economics, we refer to the trickle-down theory as that process whereas we provide tax cuts to large corporations in order for the money to trickle down to the workers (arguments for the credibility of this theory are left out of this book). Thus, in logic, we will impute a similar strategy for understanding the *subalternate* relation. In this sense, truth trickles down from the universals. So, if "A" is true, then so too is "I" true. If "E" is true, then so too is "O" true. In other words, if the universal is true, then so too must the existential be true. It is impossible for the universal to be true, and the existential to be false. However, we are not able to move the truth of the existential to the truth of the universal. For that seems to be lingering in the realm of a *hasty generalization* (quite similar although *hasty generalization* is an informal fallacy). We can, however, move the falsity of the existential to the falsity of the universal. So, if "I" is false, then so too is "A" false. If it is not the case that "Some S are P," then surely it cannot be the case that "All S are P."

Illicit subalternation involves performing a wrong inference on the *subalternate* relation. Illicit subalternation includes moving from a true existential to a true universal, and from a false universal to a false existential.

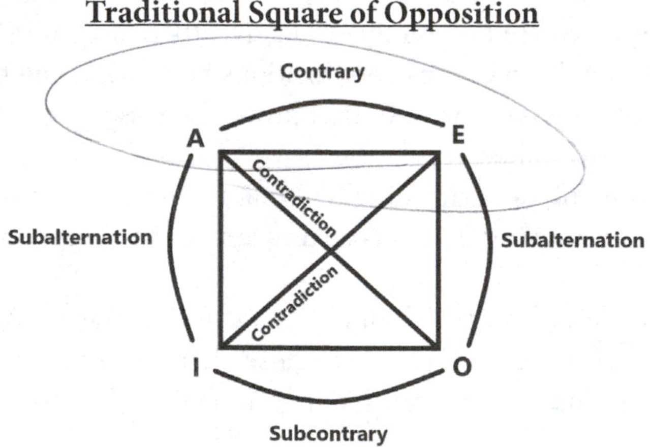

Figure created by Bradley Wakefield.

Existential Fallacy is committed under the Aristotelian system if and only if the *contrary, subcontrary*, or *subalternate* are used to draw an inference about things that do not exist. So, Aristotle will allow for any perimeter move only if the subject term actually exists. You cannot perform any of the three moves when the subject term belongs to the empty set. Again, all of these arguments include a universal premise and an existential conclusion.

All dogs are mammals.	Boole: Invalid, existential fallacy
Therefore, some dogs are mammals	Aristotle: Valid

All wizards who cast spells are malicious creatures.	Boole: Invalid, existential fallacy
Therefore, some wizards who cast spells are malicious creatures.	Aristotle: Invalid, existential fallacy

Exercise 5.3

5.3.1 *Directions:* Determine the truth-values of the other three categorical propositions. Use the traditional square of opposition to determine the values. If undetermined, then write "U"; otherwise, write "T" or "F."

*1. "A" is true.

2. "E" is false.

3. "I" is false.

4. "O" is true.

5. "E" is true.

6. "O" is false.

7. "I" is true.

8. "A" is false.

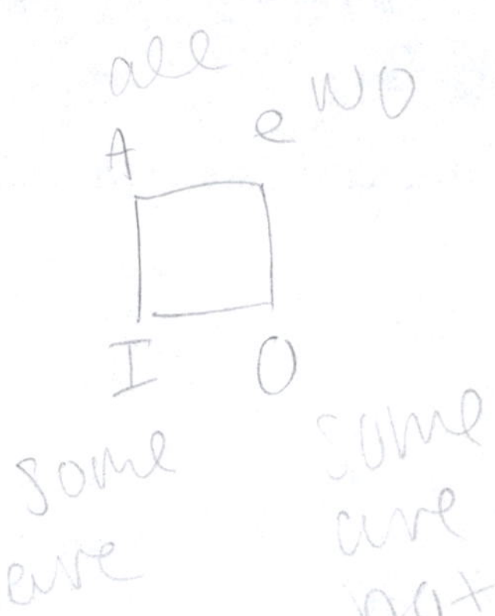

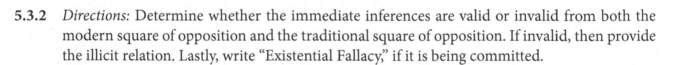

5.3.2 *Directions:* Determine whether the immediate inferences are valid or invalid from both the modern square of opposition and the traditional square of opposition. If invalid, then provide the illicit relation. Lastly, write "Existential Fallacy," if it is being committed.

*1. No musicals are operas. Therefore, it is false that all musicals are operas.

2. All dinosaurs are extinct. Therefore, some dinosaurs are extinct.

3. Some universities are more prestigious than other institutions. Therefore, some universities are not more prestigious than other institutions.

4. Some genetically modified organisms are not damaging to the consumer. Therefore, it is false that some genetically modified organisms are damaging to the consumer.

5. It is false that all wine connoisseurs are sommeliers. Therefore, some wine connoisseurs are sommeliers.

6. It is false that no statements are sentences. Therefore, all statements are sentences.

7. Some non-seasoned woods are not ready to burn. Therefore, no non-seasoned woods are ready to burn.

8. All anthropomorphic beings are human-like in form. Therefore, it is false that no anthropomorphic beings are human-like in form.

4. Equivalencies

A group of statements is said to be equivalent if and only if they express the same meaning and hence have the same truth-value. In this next section, we will explore three equivalencies that may be performed on all of the standard-form categorical propositions. In doing so, we will use Venn diagrams to determine if the new statement is logically equivalent to the original statement. The three equivalencies that we will focus our attention on are *conversion, obversion*, and *contraposition*.

Conversion involves only one step, switch the subject term and the predicate term. Once this equivalency has been done on each standard-form proposition, we will have four new statements, some of which are equivalent to the original and some of which are not. Once we complete the Venn diagrams, we will readily notice that the "A" statement is not logically equivalent. Since the "A" proposition is directional (as explained in an earlier section), we see that you cannot switch the subject term and the predicate term and retain the same meaning. "All cats are animals" is not equivalent to saying "All animals are cats." The reason for this is in part due to sufficient and necessary conditions. If you have the sufficient condition, then certainly you can extrapolate the necessary condition. However, just because you have the necessary condition, does not mean that you can posit the sufficient condition. "E" statement functions differently from the "A" statement. "E" is not directional and since it implies that the subject class and the predicate class are excluded from one another, then order does not matter. "No cats are cups" is logically equivalent to saying "No cups are cats." Thus, you may perform a conversion on an "E" statement and retain the same meaning. "I" is quite similar to "E" in the sense that we are saying that a part of the subject class is included in part of the predicate class. Since a part is in part, it appears as though this is not a directional claim. "Some dogs are fluffy animals" is logically equivalent to saying "Some fluffy animals are dogs." It may come to no surprise that "O" is quite similar to "A" because of the directional implication. Once we switch the subject term and the predicate term, we will readily notice that these are not logically equivalent. "Some professors are not pompous people" is not logically equivalent to saying "Some pompous people are not professors." Although we may be inclined to draw that inference, logic alone cannot make that leap. That is not to say, there is no truth-value for the new statement, but merely that logic alone cannot tell you the truth-value.

Illicit conversion is committed when you draw an inference from *conversion* on an "A" or "O" statement.

Look at the following Venn diagrams that show a *conversion* on each for the four categorical propositions below:

All S are P

S P

All P are S

S P

No S are P

No P are S

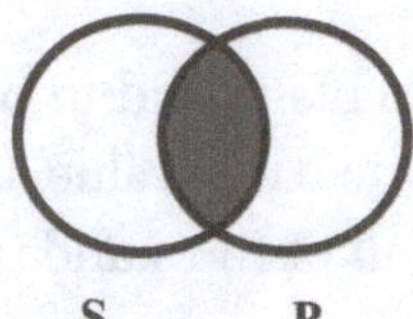

Some S are P

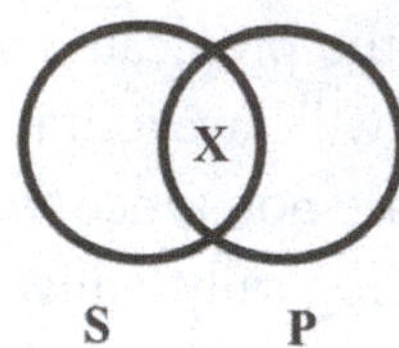

Some P are S

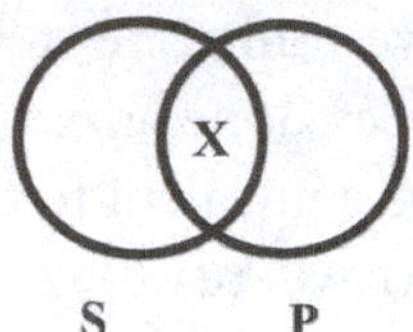

Some S are not P

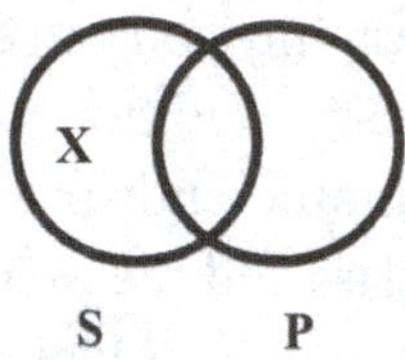

Some P are not S

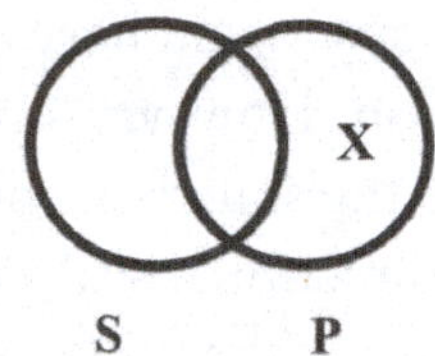

Figures created by Bradley Wakefield.

Obversion involves two steps: (1) change the quality, but not the quantity, and (2) replace the predicate with its term complement. The term complement requires the negative prefix before it. Thus, the word "book" would become "non-book," and similarly "non-book" would become "non-non-book" or "book" (rule of double negation). Upon completion of the Venn diagrams, we will readily see that all of the new statements are logically equivalent to the original statements. The change in quality along with the term complement for the predicate make it appear as though a double negation has occurred. The copula and the negative prefix are syntactically different, but for all intents and purposes, we can say that tend to behave like a double negation. There is no *illicit obversion* because each new statement is logically equivalent to the original.

Look at the following Venn diagrams that show an *obversion* on each for the four categorical propositions below:

All S are P

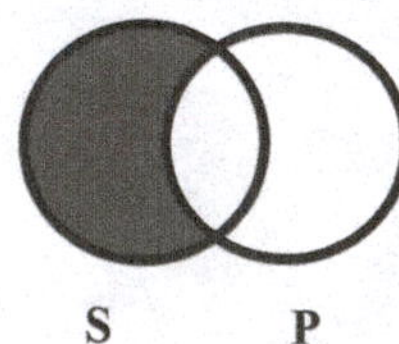

No S are non P

No S are P

All S are non P

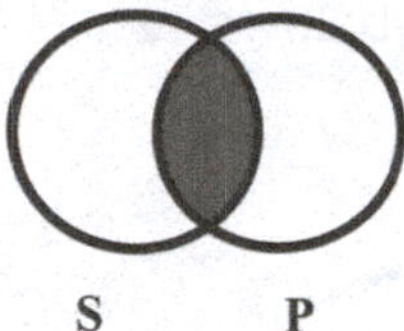

Some S are P

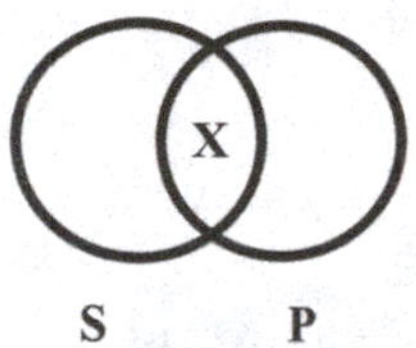

Some S are not non P

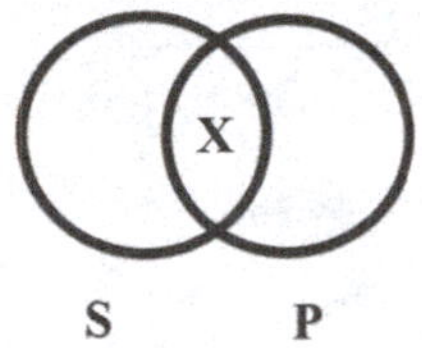

Some S are not P

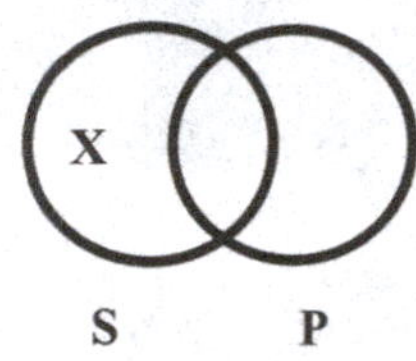

Some S are non P

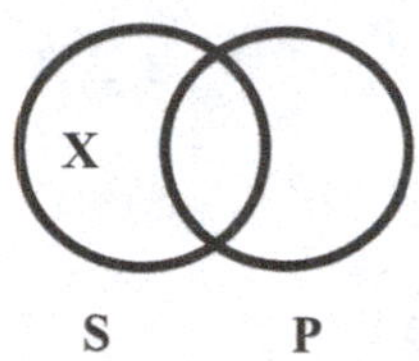

Figures created by Bradley Wakefield.

Contraposition involves two steps: (1) switch the subject term, and the predicate term, and (2) replace the subject term, and the predicate term with their term complements. In other words, flip both and negate both. Upon inspection of the Venn diagram, we will notice that the *contraposed* "A" statement is logically equivalent to the original statement. All of the *non-P*, which is everything outside the *P* circle, is a *non-S*. So, we must shade the entirety of the left apple. This diagram is logically equivalent to the original statement. The *contrapose* of "E" is not logically equivalent. This new statement is saying that there are no *non-P* and no *non-S*, which is implying that everything is an *S* or a *P*. However, this says nothing about the relationship between the subject term and the predicate term. It has only shaded all of the negative space outside both of the circles. The contrapose of "I" has a similar implication to the *contrapose* of "E." There exists a *non-P* that is also a *non-S*. That means there exists a *non-S* and *non-P*, which is outside both of the circles. This new statement if referring to an entity outside of the subject term and predicate term. That is not what the original statement is expressing, and that is why the new statement is not logically equivalent. The *contrapose* of "O" is logically equivalent to the original statement. There exists a *non-P* that is not a *non-S*. If it were a *non-S*, then the Venn diagram would look the same as the *contrapose* of "I," but it says that it is not a *non-S*. The denial of a *non-S* implies that it is indeed an *S*. Thus, it says that there exists a *non-P* that is an *S* and this is logically equivalent to saying that there exists an *S* that is not a *P*.

Illicit contraposition is committed when you draw an inference from *contraposition* on an "E" or "I" statement.

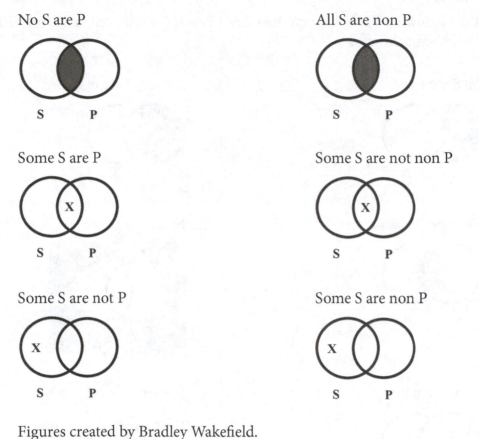

Look at the following Venn diagrams that show a *contraposition* on each for the four categorical propositions below:

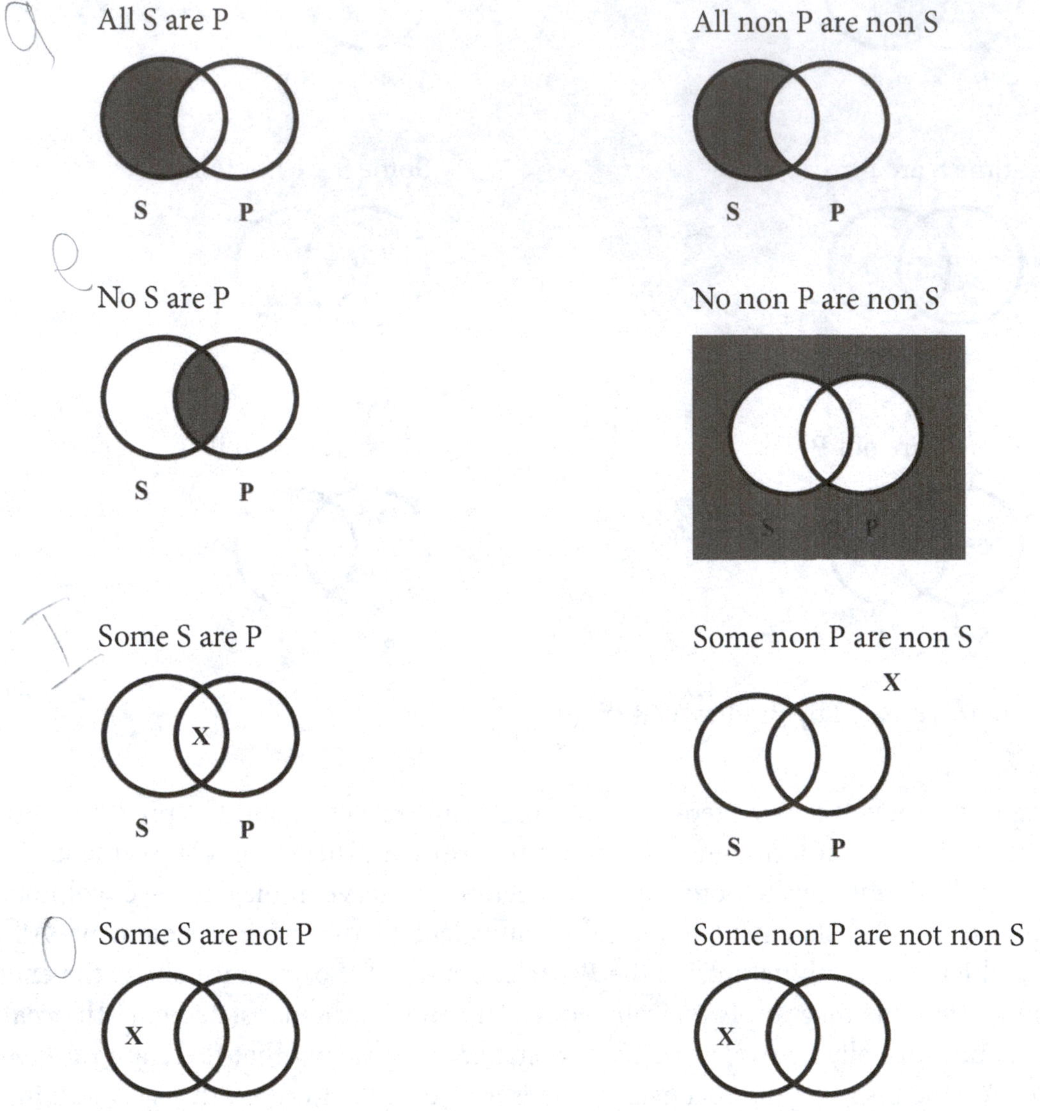

Figures created by Bradley Wakefield.

Exercise 5.4

5.4.1 *Directions:* Complete the following equivalencies on each original statement. Determine the new statement and the new truth-value. If it is an illicit move, then the new truth-value is undetermined. If the new statement is logically equivalent, then the new statement has the same truth-value as the original. The given truth-values are in italics.

Original Statement	New Statement	Truth-Value
1. Some S are non-P. *F* (conv.)		
2. All S are P. *T* (obv.)		
*3. No non-S are non-P. *T* (cont.)		
4. Some S are not non-P. *F* (obv.)		
5. All non-S are non-P. *T* (cont.)		

5.4.2 *Directions:* Complete the following equivalencies on each original statement. Determine which logical equivalency is being used when comparing the original statement and the new statement. Also, determine the truth-value of the new statement. If it is an illicit move, then the new truth-value is undetermined. If the new statement is logically equivalent, then the new statement has the same truth-value as the original. The given truth-values are in italics.

Original Statement	New Statement	Logical Equivalence	Truth-Value
1. Some non-S are non-P. *T*	Some non-P are non-S.		
2. All S are non-P. *F*	No S are P.		
3. No non-S are P. *T*	No non-P are S.		
4. Some non-S are not non-P. *F*	Some non-S are P.		
5. Some S are P. *T*	Some non-P are non-S.		

5.4.3 *Directions:* Determine whether the following arguments are valid or invalid. Use the three logical equivalencies to determine the validity. If an illicit move is being committed, then name it.

*1. All students are inquisitive learners.

Therefore, all inquisitive learners are students.

2. No unconscionable contracts are obligatory for people to follow.

Therefore, all unconscionable contracts are non-obligatory for people to follow.

3. Some video games are excessively violent depictions.

   Therefore, some non-excessively violent depictions are non-video games.

4. Some dog treats are not components of a well-balanced diet.

   Therefore, some components of a well-balanced diet are not dog treats.

5. No pine trees are maple trees.

   Therefore, no non-maple trees are non-pine trees.

6. Some sport utility vehicles are excellent off-road machines.

   Therefore, some sport utility vehicles are not non-excellent off-road machines.

7. No construction boots are flip-flops.

   Therefore, no flip-flops are construction boots.

8. Some distant stars are not entities visible to the naked eye.

   Therefore, some entities non-visible to the naked eye are not non-distant stars.

5. Categorical Proofs

Imagine that you have to travel through a series of locked doors. Each door requires that you use a key. You may not skip any of the doors. Thus, the order would need to be door 1, door 2, door 3, etc. You have a key ring with six different keys on it. Some keys may open more than one door, some keys may open only one door, and some keys may not open any doors. Each new door requires that you go through all of your keys to see which one unlocks it. So, the six keys that you have are: *contrary*, *subcontrary*, *subalternation*, *conversion*, *obversion*, and *contraposition*. The goal in this next section is to see how well you know these perimeter moves and logical equivalencies to draw further inferences. Look at the following examples below:

All politicians are smooth talking con artists.

Therefore, some smooth talking con artists are politicians.

1. All P are S (T)
2. Some P are S (T) *subalternation*

∴ Some S are P (T) *conversion*

No paintings that do not contain people are masterpieces.

Therefore, some non-masterpieces are not paintings that contain people.

1. No non-P are M (T)
2. Some non-P are not M (T) *subalternation*

∴ Some non-M are not P (T) *contraposition*

All electroencephalograms are recordings of brain activity.

Therefore, it is false that all recordings of brain activity are non-electroencephalograms.

1. All E are R (T)
2. No E are R (F) *contrary*
3. No R are E (F) *conversion*

∴ It is false that all R are non-E *obversion*

Exercise 5.5

5.5.1 *Directions:* Complete the following proofs using *contrary, subcontrary, subalternation, conversion, obversion,* and *contraposition.*

1. It is false that some records are digital recordings.

   Therefore, all records are analogue recordings.

2. All condescending rebuttals are offensive remarks.

   Therefore, some offensive remarks are uncondescending rebuttals.

*3. No pieces of fictional writing are true stories.

   Therefore, some true stories are not pieces of fictional writing.

4. It is false that some video games are unentertaining past times.

   Therefore, some entertaining past times are video games.

5. It is false that no unremarkable sport outings are enjoyable events.

   Therefore, some enjoyable events are not remarkable sport outings.

6. It is false that some ill-conceived mathematical equations are not helpful practice problems.

   Therefore, some helpful practice problems are not well-conceived mathematical equations.

7. It is false that some reptiles are not tetrapods.

   Therefore, it is false that all tetrapods are non-reptiles.

8. It is false that some black holes are not things detectable with our current technology.

   Therefore, it is false that all things undetectable with our current technology are black holes.

6. Categorical Syllogisms

Categorical syllogisms consist of three categorical propositions all of which must be standard-form categorical propositions. Aristotle is the first philosopher to recognize the form of a categorical syllogism. According to Aristotle, when two categorical propositions are linked together (inferential connection), a third proposition arises, which we call the conclusion. Thus, the truth of the conclusion depends on the two premises and the link between the premises. In this section, we will learn a technique to determine the validity of categorical syllogisms.

All nurturing individuals are doctors.

Some politicians are not nurturing individuals.

Therefore, no politicians are doctors.

Let's start with the conclusion. The conclusion is always the relationship between the subject term and the predicate term. Thus, the conclusion is always the relation between *S* and *P*. The subject term of the conclusion is the minor term. The minor term is always found in the minor premise. So, the subject term will always occur in the second premise. The second premise of the argument is called the minor premise.

On the other hand, the predicate term of the conclusion is the major term. The major term always occurs in the major premise. The major premise is the first premise of the argument. So, you will readily notice that *P* will occur in the first premise (major) and *S* will occur in the second premise (minor). If we look at the example given above, then we will see that "politicians" is the minor term and occurs in the second premise. We will also note that "doctors" is the major term and occurs in the first premise. Again, the conclusion is always the relationship between the minor and the major term. An "A" statement for the conclusion is "All minor are major," an "E" statement for the conclusion is "No minor are major." The same goes for "I" and "O." An "I" as the conclusion is "Some minor are major," and "O" as the conclusion is "Some minor are not major." You should notice that there is a term that is neither the major nor is it the minor. That is what is called the middle term—*M*. The middle term occurs in both premises but not in the conclusion. The middle term provides the glue between the two premises. The middle term serves as the glue that helps bind the inferential link between the premises to derive the conclusion. So, in the example above, "nurturing individuals" is the middle term because it occurs in both premises, but not in the conclusion.

A standard-form categorical syllogism must include all of the following conditions:

1. Each statement must be a standard-form categorical proposition (A, E, I, O).
2. Each term must be used in the same sense in order to avoid equivocation.
3. The order of the premises and conclusion matters. The major premise is listed first, the minor second, and the conclusion last.

A standard-form categorical syllogism consists of three standard-form categorical propositions that make it up. So, to simplify matters, we can write the three successive letter names that make the argument. Look at the following argument below:

All cats are mammals.

All mammals are animals.

Therefore, all cats are animals.

Since all three of the statements are an "A" statement, the argument *mood* is AAA. The mood is the successive sequence of letters that make up an argument. An EOI argument would look like the following:

(1) No___ are ___

(2) Some___ are not____

∴ Some S are P

The only thing that the mood tells you is the type of categorical propositions that make the argument. However, the mood is unable to tell you the location of the major term, minor term, and middle term. For that, we must use another device. We use the *figure* to determine the location of the terms. The figure is the possible arrangement of major, minor, and middle terms. There are four possible combinations of term arrangements.

	Figure 1	Figure 2	Figure 3	Figure 4
(1)	M P	P M	M P	P M
(2)	S M	S M	M S	M S
∴	S P	S P	S P	S P

The conclusion is always the relationship between the subject and the predicate. So, the mood is necessary, but it is not sufficient. If you were given the following mood (EEO), then you would only be able to construct part of the argument.

(1) No___ are____

(2) No___ are____

∴ Some S are not P

You already know that the major term (predicate of the conclusion) must be contained in the major premise, but you do not know if it is the subject or predicate of the major premise. You now that the minor term (the subject of the conclusion) must be contained in the minor premise, but you do not know if it is the subject or predicate of the minor premise. The four figures provide you with the additional information about the location of the major, minor, and middle terms.

Look at the following arguments below:

EEO-4

(1) No P are M

(2) No M are S

∴ Some S are not P

AIE-1

(1) All M are P

(2) Some S are M

∴ No S are P

OIO-2

(1) Some P are not M

(2) Some S are M

∴ Some S are not P

IIA-3

(1) Some M are P

(2) Some M are S

∴ All S are P

It can be quite challenging to remember the four different figures. Here are two possible ways in which you might remember the four figures. The first one involves dress shirts and ties. Silk ties are very delicate objects. Cleaning silk is nearly impossible. So, if you get a stain on a silk tie, then the tie is permanently ruined. Imagine looking directly at the top of a dress shirt. The two collar flaps are straight down from the face, and then they angle back around the neck. The only thing that should be between the two collar flaps is a tie.

Moreover remember, that you need to keep everything off of the tie. If you look at the four figures, specifically the middle terms, you will notice that they are straight down in figure 2 and 3, and then angle back in figures 1 and 4. Start from the predicate of figure 2 and the subject of figure 3, and imagine drawing a line straight down to the conclusion. Then, make an angle from the bottom of figure 2 over toward figure 1. Make the line cross over both instances of the middle term. Now imagine the same thing for the other side. Once you draw the line to the bottom of figure 3, make an acute angle and continue to draw a lineup and over to figure 4 crossing over both instances of the middle term. You should be looking at two large check marks, which are the mirrored opposites of one another. The two lines that you have drawn are the edge of the shirt collar. So, the *M*s should always be along the edge of the shirt collar. For figures 1 and 4, all that you need to do now is to put the *P* at the top and the *S* below it. The confusion is usually with figures 2 and 3. Remember that you do not want anything to get on the silk tie or else it is ruined. Make sure that you put *S* and *P* on the collar and not on the tie. Keep it off the tie.

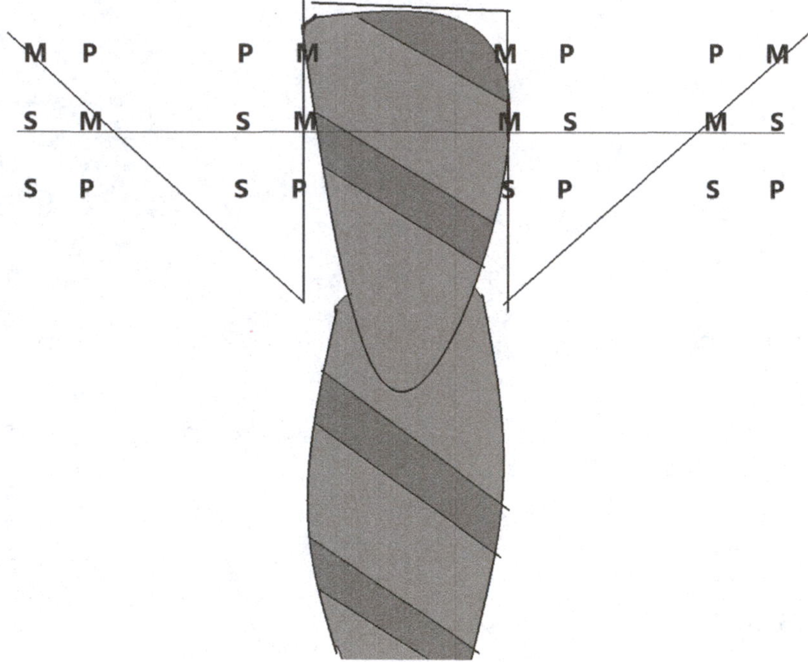

Figure created by Bradley Wakefield.

If you are not as familiar with dress shirts and ties, then maybe thinking about the *Star Wars* franchise might help. Image the *Millennium Falcon* that Han Solo and Chewbacca drive. You should, then, be able to construct a similar diagram. The *Millennium Falcon* diagram is another way to help you memorize the four figures.[1] If you were looking down on the *Millennium Falcon* from a bird's eye view, you would notice that the front of the ship looks quite similar to the edge of the collared shirt (see diagram below). For figures 2 and 3, all that you need to remember is that Han and Chewbacca do not drive the craft from outside the ship, they must be inside to do so.

[1] This idea was first proposed by Theresa Catalano-Reinhardt during a faculty development day at Macomb Community College, 2016.

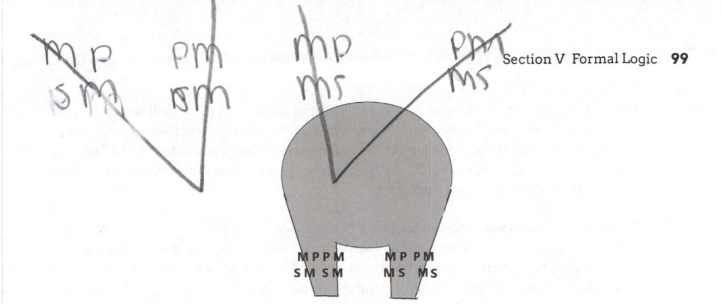

MP PM MP PM
SM SM MS MS

Figure created by Bradley Wakefield.

Testing Validity of Categorical Syllogisms

Now that we have included the middle term, the two overlapping circles will no longer suffice. We must include the third circle for all categorical syllogisms.

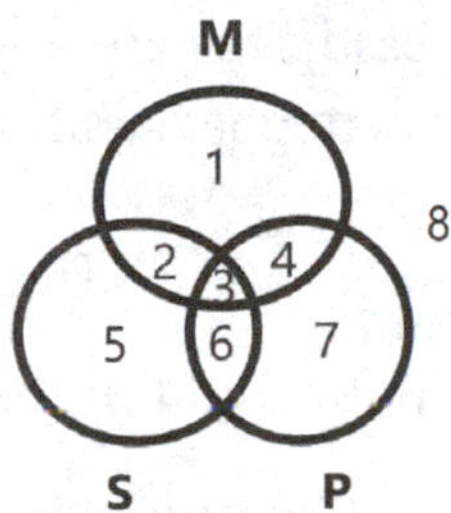

Figure created by Bradley Wakefield.

There are some rules when it comes to constructing Venn diagrams for arguments.

(i) You should only mark, by shading or placing an "X," for the premises. The premises should imply the truth of the conclusion, so the markings should draw the conclusion.

(ii) Shade the universal propositions first and then place the "X" for the existential propositions. Universals shade all of the negative space, so it is important to get rid of the negative space before you make a positive assertion by the "X."

(iii) Each of the four propositions asserts a relation between two terms. Focus on the two terms that the proposition is referring to.

(iv) Shade the entire area in question. If you are to shade the left apple, then shade the entire left apple. If you are to shade the football, then shade the entire football.

(v) Now that there are three circles, the left apple, right apple, and football have been divided into parts. So, if one of those areas are shaded, then put the "X" in the open area.

(vi) If neither one of the parts is shaded, then put the "X" on the line. It would be completely arbitrary to place the "X" one area over the other. In other words, you have no special insight into the nature of the argument that allows you to put the "X" in a specific area. By putting the "X" on the line, you are signifying that you lack the required information to place it in an area.

We begin with the Boolean system because it is much more simplified than the Aristotelian system. Imagine that you are looking out of your bedroom window. Suppose further that you took some masking tape and framed out a small square over your window. Now when you look through that smaller square, you are restricted in an absolute sense. In fact, even looking out of the entire window is quite restricting. I want you to imagine that the smaller square is the Boolean view, and the entire window is the Aristotelian view. It should be evident that if you can see something out of the smaller square (Boolean), then you can see it out of the entire window (Aristotelian) as well. The converse is not true. There may be things that you can see out of the whole window, but you cannot see it out of the smaller window. Finally, some things are outside of both the smaller window and the larger window. There are three possible ways to classify categorical syllogisms. First is that if it is unconditionally valid for Boole, then it is valid for Aristotle as well. Second, the argument could be invalid for Boole, but conditionally valid for Aristotle (the condition being that if the subject actually exists). Lastly, the argument could be invalid for Boole and Aristotle. Here are the three ways in which you might classify all 256 categorical syllogisms:

(i)	(ii)	(iii)
B: Unconditionally Valid	B: Invalid E.F. (existential fallacy)	B: Invalid
A: Valid	A: Conditionally Valid (if subject exists)	A: Invalid

In this first section, we will be classifying arguments that are either option (i) or option (iii)—we will come to option (ii) when we test from the Aristotelian system.

AAE-1

(1) All M are P

(2) All S are M

∴ No S are P

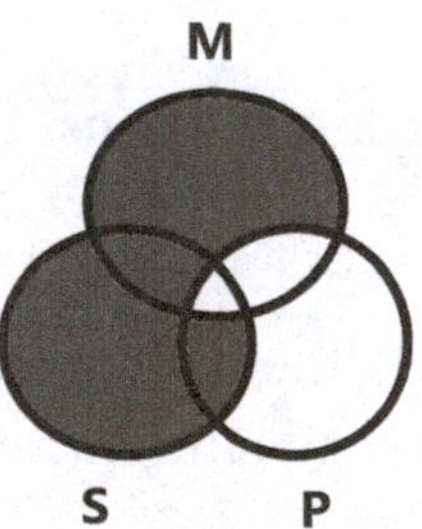

Figure created by Bradley Wakefield.

B: Invalid

A: Invalid

IAI-3

(1) Some M are P

(2) All M are S

∴ Some S are P

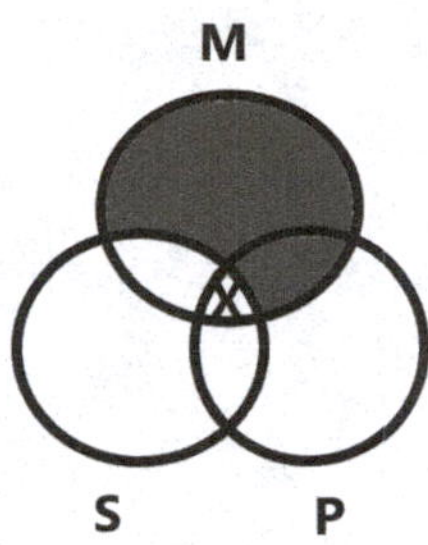

Figure created by Bradley Wakefield.

B: Unconditionally Valid

A: Valid

EIO-4

(1) No P are M

(2) Some M are S

∴ Some S are not P

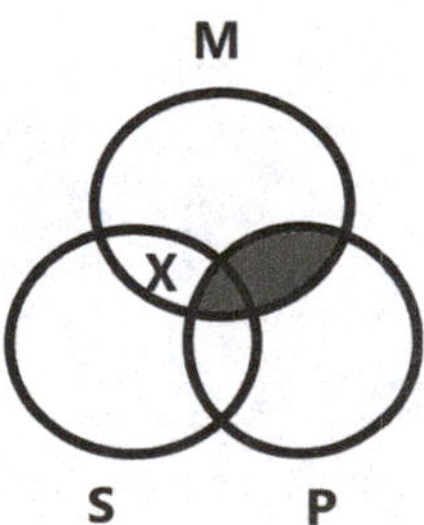

Figure created by Bradley Wakefield.

B: Unconditionally Valid

A: Valid

OAO-1

(1) Some M are not P

(2) All S are M

∴ Some S are not P

Figure created by Bradley Wakefield.

B: Invalid

A: Invalid

AAA-4

(1) All P are M

(2) All M are S

∴ All S are P

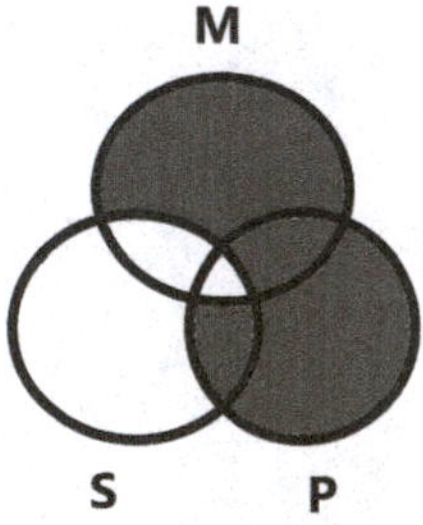

Figure created by Bradley Wakefield.

B: Invalid

A: Invalid

IOI-2

(1) Some P are M

(2) Some S are not M

∴ Some S are P

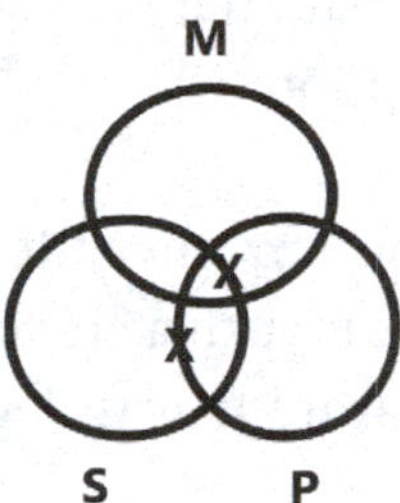

Figure created by Bradley Wakefield.

B: Invalid

A: Invalid

OEE-3

(1) Some M are not P

(2) No M are S

∴ No S are P

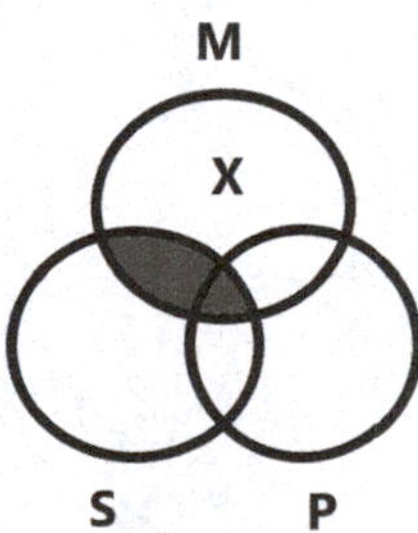

Figure created by Bradley Wakefield.

B: Invalid

A: Invalid

Now let's have a look at the Aristotelian system. It is only necessary to check it from the Aristotelian system when an existential fallacy has occurred for Boole; otherwise, it is the option (i) or (iii). The existential fallacy is committed when, and only when the argument is invalid merely because the conclusion has existential import and the premise lacks it. Such arguments have universal premises and an existential conclusion.

(i) Test the argument from the Boolean system. You will notice that the shading does not imply an "X," and thus, the argument is invalid and existential fallacy for Boole. That means that we are checking to see if the argument is option (ii).

(ii) Once the diagram is constructed from the Boolean system, check to see if there is a circle that is entirely shaded except for one area. If there is such a circle, then that is the critical term. Aristotle's particular condition that his argument is dependent upon is the critical term.

(iii) In the open area of the critical term, place an "X" with a circle around it to denote it a provisional status. Provisional here means a stand-in assumption for testing purposes.

(iv) Once you have a provisional "X," go ahead and retest the argument from the Aristotelian system. If the provisional "X" implies the conclusion, then the argument is conditionally valid as long as the critical term exists. If the provisional "X" does not imply the conclusion, then the argument is invalid according to both systems.

AAI-3

(1) All M are P

(2) All M are S

∴ Some S are P

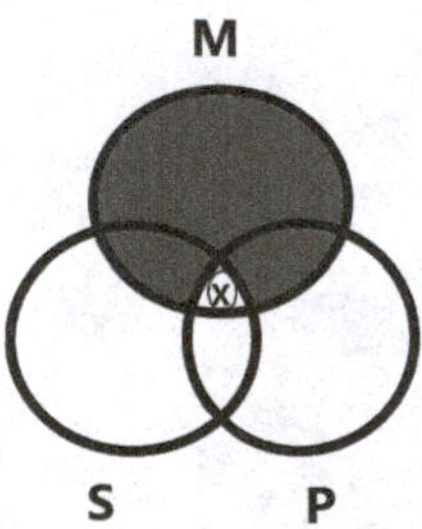

Figure created by Bradley Wakefield.

B: Invalid; Existential Fallacy

A: Conditionally Valid, if *M* exists

EAO-1

(1) No M are P

(2) All S are M

∴ Some S are not P

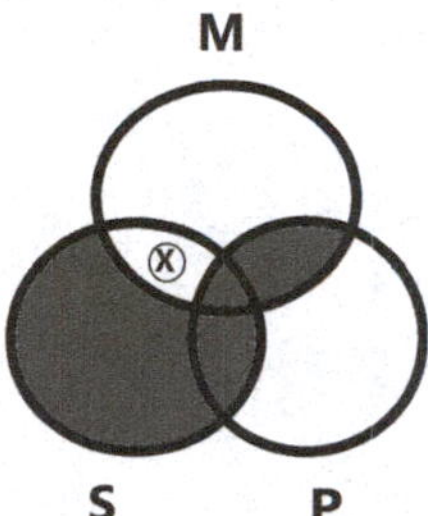

Figure created by Bradley Wakefield.

B: Invalid; Existential Fallacy

A: Conditionally Valid, if *S* exists

AEO-4

(1) All P are M

(2) No M are S

∴ Some S are not P

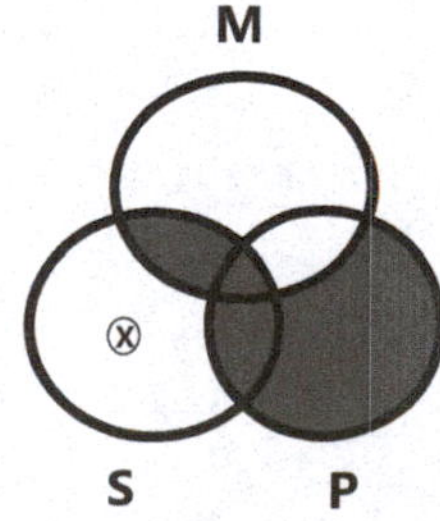

Figure created by Bradley Wakefield.

B: Invalid; Existential Fallacy

A: Conditionally Valid, if *S* exists

AAO-2

(1) All P are M

(2) All S are M

∴ Some S are not P

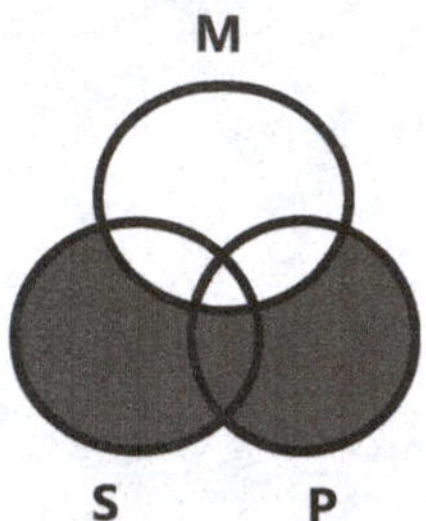

Figure created by Bradley Wakefield.

B: Invalid; Existential Fallacy

A: Invalid; Existential Fallacy

EAI-3

(1) No M are P

(2) All M are S

∴ Some S are P

Figure created by Bradley Wakefield.

B: Invalid; Existential Fallacy

A: Invalid; Existential Fallacy

Unconditionally Valid Arguments

Figure 1	Figure 2	Figure 3	Figure 4
AAA	EAE	IAI	AEE
EAE	AEE	AII	IAI
AII	EIO	OAO	EIO
EIO	AOO	EIO	

Conditionally Valid Arguments

Figure 1	Figure 2	Figure 3	Figure 4
AAI (S exists)	AEO (S exists)	AAI (M exists)	AEO (S exists)
EAO (S exists)	EAO (S exists)	EAO (M exists)	EAO (M exists)
			AAI (P exists)

Exercise 5.6

5.6.1 *Directions:* Put the following arguments into standard form. Then, determine if the argument is invalid or valid from both the Aristotelian and Boolean standpoint.

1. EAE-4
2. OAA-2
3. IEI-3
4. OOO-1
5. EAI-1
6. AOI-2
7. AEE-4
8. IIA-1
9. OAI-3
10. EAO-2

5.6.2 *Directions:* Put the following arguments into standard form. Then, determine if the argument is invalid or valid from both the Aristotelian and Boolean standpoint. Since you are provided with the content of the three terms, you should not have any conditionally valid arguments. If the subject exists, then it is valid, and if not, then it is invalid (existential fallacy).

*1. All pseudo-sciences are a complete waste of time. All holistic approaches to medicine are a complete waste of time. Therefore, all holistic approaches to medicine are pseudo-sciences.

2. All historians of antiquity are people familiar with mythology. Therefore, since some professors are historians of antiquity, some professors are people familiar with mythology.

3. All cold-brewed coffees are terrible concoctions. Since no terrible concoctions are delightful treats and some delightful treats are cold-brewed coffees.

4. All wizards with exceptional magical powers are members of Slytherin. No members of Gryffindor are wizards with exceptional magical powers. Thus, some members of Slytherin are not members of Gryffindor.

5. Some crocodiles are dinosaurs. For all aquatic reptiles are crocodiles, and some aquatic reptiles are dinosaurs.

5.6.3 *Directions:* Look at the following Venn Diagrams. Determine the premises and the conclusion of the argument. If there is not a conclusion present, then write "No conclusion." Once you have constructed the argument form, please provide the mood and figure.

1.

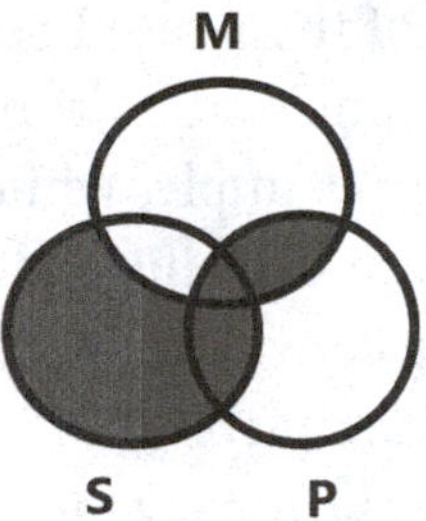

2.

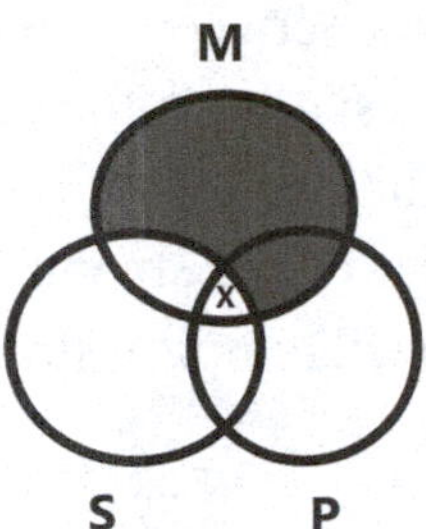

3.

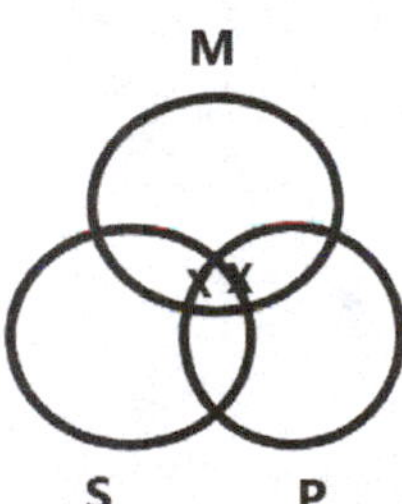

4.

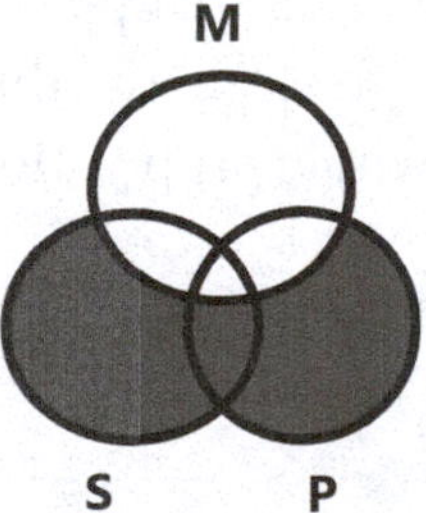

Figures created by Bradley Wakefield.

b. Sentential Logic

1. Translating Sentences

i. Abbreviations are used in your everyday lives. POTUS (President of the United States), DOJ (Department of Justice), DSO (Detroit Symphony Orchestra) are some of the primary examples that you will see. We also use them when we are in a rush. For example, while composing a text message, you might find it much easier and quicker to use LOL instead of writing "Laughing out loud." We use abbreviations to simplify what is being conveyed. So, an abbreviation may serve as a symbol to stand for components of a term (descriptive phrase, common name, or proper name). Sentential logic functions in a similar way. Ordinary language often obscures the internal structure of an argument. Hence, abbreviations are used to expose the internal structure in order to test the validity of an argument. We use symbolic letters to represent whole sentences. A categorical syllogism expresses the relation between terms, whereas sentential logic expresses the relation between whole sentences. To test a form for validity, you need to, first of all, put the argument into argument form. Again, the content of an argument can often masquerade the structure of an argument making it appear either stronger than it is or weaker than it is. Once the argument is put into proper form, we will employ similar tactics for testing validity as you have done in earlier sections of this book.

The primary goal in this section is to break the sentences into their smaller components and write the arguments out in symbolic notation. The smallest component of an argument is called a *simple* statement. A simple statement functions much like a categorical syllogism. It has a subject and predicate relation. Look at the following examples below:

Logic is difficult.

Summer break is short.

Dogs are friendly.

Pompeii was destroyed in 79 AD.

Symbolic notation can be utilized here to simplify the sentences. You can use uppercase letters to represent the entire sentence. The first sentence, *L*, the second sentence, *S*, the third, *D*, and the fourth, *P*. Each of these four letters is being used to notate the whole proposition.

A *compound* statement—much like in chemistry—is a group of at least one simple statement and an operator. Look at the following examples below:

It is not the case that Logic is difficult.

Summer break is short, and classes begin soon.

Either dogs are friendly, or cats are fluffy.

If Mt. Vesuvius did in fact erupt, then Pompeii was destroyed in 79 AD.

A person is happy if and only if they have completed that which will make them happy.

All five of these examples involve at least one *simple* statement and an *operator*. So, the symbolic notation for the examples are as follows:

It is not the case that L.

S and C.

Either D or C.

If M, then P.

H if and only if C.

ii. The last piece of symbolic notation is reserved for *operators*. Operators are needed to connect simple statements. The operators are *negation, conjunction, disjunction, conditional*, and *biconditional*. Here is a table for the operators.

Operator	**Name**	**Ordinary Language**
~	Tilde	Negation: not, it is not the case that
•	Dot	Conjunction: and, but, moreover, also
∨	Wedge	Disjunction: Either/or
⊃	Horseshoe/Superset	Conditional: If, then, only if, if
≡	Triple bar	Biconditional: if and only if

Now you may complete the symbolic notation on the above examples using the uppercase letters and the operators.

~L

S • C

D ∨ C

M ⊃ P

H ≡ C

You could have a long proposition that includes more than one operator. For example, if the ice cream truck comes by my house and I catch them before they leave, then I will order an éclair bar or a push pop. In this example, we have conjunction, conditional, and a disjunction. The most critical operator in this sentence is conditional. The conditional statement is the central operator that is joining all of the simple statements. The central operator that does this is called the *main operator*. The *main operator* has all of the simple statements within its scope. So, the notation, for example, is as follows:

(I • C) ⊃ (E ∨ P)

There are a few translations that need some further explanation. The first one has to do with conditionals. Look at the following examples:

If we leave our vehicle running while we shop, then plenty of gas will be wasted.

Plenty of gas will be wasted, if we leave our vehicle running.

Plenty of gas will be wasted only if we leave our vehicle running.

The first example is rather straightforward. If the antecedent is satisfied, then the consequent follows. The second example provides the consequent if the antecedent is satisfied. The third example is somewhat confusing. You might be inclined to think of it the same as the second example. Think of the word "only" for a moment. The word "only" refers to exclusivity or necessity. That being the case, the phrase "only if" is preceding that which is exclusive or necessary. Whichever term follows the phrase "only if" must be necessary. Since we know that conditional expresses the relation between a sufficient and a necessary condition; that means the second part is the necessary condition. Remember, if sufficient, then necessary. So, "we leave our vehicle running" is denoting the consequent and "plenty of gas will be wasted" is the antecedent. Thus, leaving our vehicle running is a necessary condition for plenty of gas being wasted, notwithstanding the truth or falsity of such claims.

There are many different ways to express a conditional statement beyond the above mentioned. Look at the following examples of conditional statements below:

P provided that Q $\quad Q \supset P$

P on condition that Q $\quad Q \supset P$

P given that Q $\quad Q \supset P$

P in case Q $\quad Q \supset P$

P implies Q $\quad P \supset Q$

P is sufficient for Q $\quad P \supset Q$

P is necessary for Q $\quad Q \supset P$

P unless Q $\quad {\sim}Q \supset P$

The next set of translations in need of explanation includes the variations of conjunctions. Look at the following examples of conjunction statements below:

Not either Socrates or Plato is a sophist. $\quad {\sim}(S \vee P)$

Neither Socrates nor Plato is a sophist.	$\sim(S \vee P)$
Both Socrates and Plato are not sophists.	$\sim(S \vee P)$
Not both Socrates and Plato are sophists.	$\sim(S \bullet P)$
Either Socrates or Plato is not a sophist.	$\sim S \vee \sim P$

The first example states that it is not the case that either this or that. So, this is a negation of a disjunction. The second example states that it is not this or that, which means that $\sim(S \vee P)$ is equivalent to $\sim S \bullet \sim P$. These equivalencies are called De Morgan's Laws. The third example states that it is not the case that either this or that. All three of these compound statements are logically equivalent. However, the last two are different. The fourth one states it is not the case that this and that. This is a negated conjunction. Similarly, as we saw with the other equivalencies of De Morgan's Laws, either this or that is not the case, and is not this or not that, which is equivalent to $\sim(S \bullet P)$.

Sentences must have proper syntax in order to avoid confusion and ambiguity. Semantics has to do with meanings of words or other symbols. The syntax is the rules for the formation of grammatical sentences in a language. Symbolic notation requires proper syntax to avoid confusion and ambiguity. When the symbolic notation has proper syntax, we refer to the notation as a well-formed formula (WFF). Some of the rules for a WFF includes: simple statement must be combined with an operator, two operators cannot combine the same two simples, most operators cannot precede an individual letter, parentheses and brackets are used to group together certain simple statements, and an operator cannot succeed an individual letter. Although this list of rules is not exhaustive, it should be a decent start.

Here are some examples of WFFS:

$\sim S \vee P$

$(S \supset P) \bullet \sim M$

$[\sim M \equiv (P \vee M)] \supset (S \bullet M)$

$(P \bullet S) \supset \sim[(M \vee M) \equiv P]$

$\sim S$

Here are some examples of non-WFFS:

$P\sim$

PS

$\equiv \bullet S(S \bullet M)$

$(MP)M \supset S\sim S \vee P$

$[(P \supset S) \supset S]\sim[P \vee (M \vee M)]$

Exercise 5.7

5.7.1 *Directions:* Put the following statements into symbolic notation. Use uppercase letters and the symbolic notation for the operators.

1. Logic is a difficult course.
2. I have a final exam tomorrow, and I have to babysit my siblings.
3. Either Steven is the most obnoxious person, or he is a skeptic.
4. The event was completed, but some of the stands were still open.
5. If the election goes as planned, then we will see a massive shift in political leadership.
6. You will get an "A" in this course if and only if you successfully complete all of the required work.
7. It is not the case that your perceptions are your reality.
8. I will not eat my dinner unless you eat dinner.
9. Not both ethics and logic meet on Mondays.
10. Logic will not be offered next year unless the philosophy of mind is offered.
11. Either logic or ethics meet on Mondays, given that both metaphysics and philosophy of religion meet on Tuesdays.
12. The call for papers is a necessary condition for the conference this fall.

*13. Drinking a tall glass of iced tea on a hot summer day is a sufficient condition for quenching your thirst.

14. It is not the case that both logic being offered in the fall implies that philosophy of science will be offered in the winter and ethics being offered in the spring implies that philosophy of women will be offered in the summer.
15. Neither a borrower nor a lender be.[2]

5.7.2 *Directions:* Determine whether the following statements are WFFs. If so, then write "WFF," and if not, then write "non-WFF."

1. ~G
2. ~(H~K)

[2] Shakespeare, William. *Hamlet*, edited by George Richard Hibbard, Oxford UP, 2008, Act 1, Scene 3, p. 3.

3. F~
4. ~~~B
5. L • N~
6. JK
7. ~[(G ≡ I) • (~T ∨ N~)]
8. (R ∨ • ~D) ⊃ (S ∨ W)
9. U ⊃ [(R ∨ A) ⊃ (T ≡ V)]
10. ~[(T • G) ∨ (T ∨ ~G)] ⊃ (B ≡ ~W)

2. Truth Functionality

Truth Functionality is when the truth-values of the simple statements and the operators collectively allow us to derive further truth-values. So, the truth-value of a compound statement is a function of the truth-values of the simple statements in combination with rules for the operators. Truth-values of simple statements and the operators determine the truth values of more massive sequences.

A truth table is all of the possible arrangements of truth-values for a set of simple statements to determine compound truth-values. Truth tables exhaust all of the possibilities of truth. In other words, there should not be any other options for truth once completed. There are two tables used to show all of the possible truth-values for the five operators. In classical logic, we adhere to bivalency, for example, truth and falsity. So, the truth tables used in this book are only for propositions that are true or false. Three-valued logic requires different truth tables, and is outside the scope of this class.

Negation Table

P	~P
T	F
F	T

Operator Table

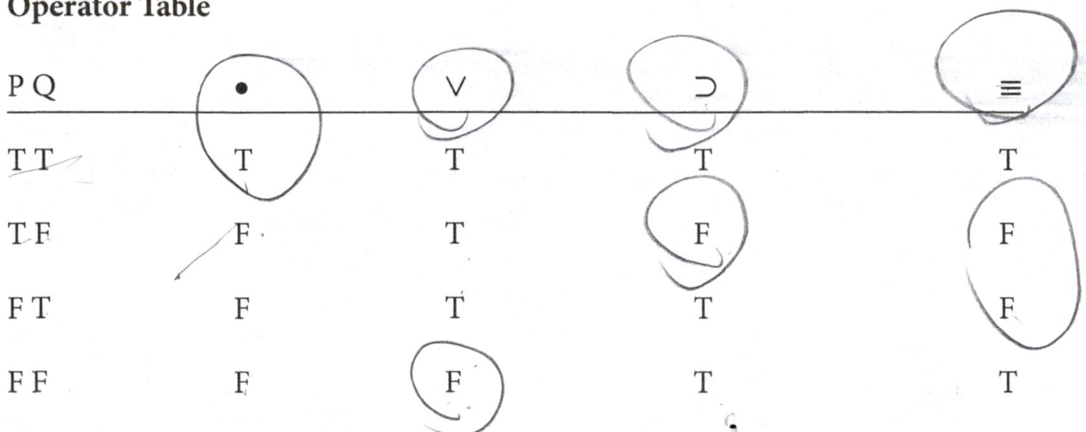

P Q	•	∨	⊃	≡
T T	T	T	T	T
T F	F	T	F	F
F T	F	T	T	F
F F	F	F	T	T

Conjunctions are true only in cases where both of the conjuncts are true; otherwise, it is false. Disjunctions are true as long as one of the disjuncts is true; otherwise, it is false. A conditional is only false when the antecedent is true, and the consequent is false; otherwise, it is true. Lastly, a biconditional is true when both of the simple statements share the same truth-value; otherwise, it is false. To understand the truth-values for compound statements that are biconditional, you need to understand the truth-values for conditionals. A biconditional is a conjunction between both directions of a conditional (*if* and *only if*). Remember, P if Q is translated into Q ⊃ P and P only if Q is translated into P ⊃ Q. So, the biconditional P ≡ Q is the more massive conjunction of [(Q ⊃ P) • (P ⊃ Q)].

Now you can compute sizeable compound truth-values when you are provided the truth-values for the simple statements. Remember, the truth-values of the simple statements in combination with the meanings of the operators allow you to determine the truth-values of compound statements.

In mathematics, we use an order of operations (PEMDAS). We use an order of operations in logic as well. To compute a great sequence, you begin with the innermost individual letter and work to the outermost. So, the rules are as follows:

(i) Replace the individual letters with their respective truth-values.

(ii) Negate individual letters preceded by the tilde.

(iii) Compute the operators joining letters.

(iv) Compute the innermost parentheses.

(v) Negate outside the parentheses.

(vi) Compute the innermost brackets.

(vii) Negate outside the brackets.

(viii) Continue this process until you have completed the whole sequence.

Let A, B, C be true, and D, E, G be false. Now that you have the truth-values of the simple statements and the meanings for the operators, you should be able to compute the large sequences.

(B • C) ⊃ E

(T • T) ⊃ F

T ⊃ F

<u>F</u>

~E ≡ (B ∨ A)

F ≡ (T ∨ T)

T ≡ T

<u>T</u>

~[(G ∨ A) • ~(B ⊃ C)] ≡ (D • ~E)

~[(F ∨ T) • ~(T ⊃ T)] ≡ (F • F)

(F • T)

~[T • T] ≡ F

~[T • F] ≡ F

F ≡ F

T ≡ F

<u>F</u>

Exercise 5.8

5.8.1 *Directions:* Indicate whether the following statements are true or false.

1. Truth-functionality is that the truth-values of the simple statements and the operators are a function of the truth values of the compound statements.
2. Truth tables are constructed using trivalency.
3. If a statement is negated, then it is automatically false.
4. Negation is distributed much like in mathematics.
5. Truth-values for compound statements are constructed from the outermost to the innermost.
6. The first step for computing the truth-values of compound statements is to replace the letters with their respective truth-values.
7. The final step in computing the truth-values of compound statements is the main operator.
8. Biconditionals are true if and only if the simple statements share the same truth-value.

5.8.2 *Directions:* Assume that *J, K, L* are true and that *M, N, O* are false. Compute the truth-values for the following compound statements:

1. $\sim M$
2. $L \supset N$
3. $\sim M \vee (L \bullet J)$
4. $\sim(J \equiv M) \supset [O \bullet (J \vee L)]$
5. $[\sim[(N \bullet \sim K) \vee (J \equiv L)] \supset \sim[(O \equiv \sim N) \bullet (\sim L \vee \sim M)]]$
6. $\sim[\sim[\sim(L \vee K) \supset \sim O] \equiv [M \equiv [(J \vee N) \vee \sim(L \supset \sim K)]]] \equiv \sim[(J \vee K) \equiv \sim O]$

Truth Tables for Statements Without Given Truth-Values

When you are not provided with the truth-values of the simple statements, you must construct a truth table underneath the compound statement. There is a relationship between the number of simple statements and the number of lines for the truth value. When there is only one simple statement, the truth table has two lines. When there are two simple statements, the truth table has four lines, and when there are three simple statements, the truth table has eight lines. You should recognize that there is a pattern here. $L = 2^n$ is the formula that expresses the relation between the number of simple statements and the number of lines on the truth table. The number of lines, L, is equal to 2 to the *n* power. The *n* denotes the number of simple statements.

(D ⊃ C)	•	~C
T T T	F	F T
T F F	F	T F
F T T	F	F T
F T F	T	T F

(A	•	~G)	∨	~(B	≡	G)
T	F	F T	F	F T	T	T
T	F	F T	T	T F	F	T
T	T	T F	T	T T	F	F
T	T	T F	T	F F	T	F
F	F	F T	F	F T	T	T
F	F	F T	T	T F	F	T
F	F	T F	T	T T	F	F
F	F	T F	F	F F	T	F

There are three ways in which you may classify statements, *tautology*, *self-contradiction*, and *contingent*. A statement is said to a *tautology* if and only if the column under the main operator is all true. In this case, the truth-values of the simple statements do not matter, because regardless of those truth-values the whole statement is true. The same may be said for *self-contradictions*. In this case, the truth-values of the simple statements do not matter, because regardless of those truth-values the whole statement is false. However, a *contingent* statement does depend on the truth-values of the simple statements. A *contingent* statement has at least one truth and at least one false line under the main operator.

You may also compare two statements side by side to see if they are logically equivalent—similar to what you did with categorical propositions—or if they are contradictory. Look at the following examples below:

~(S • P)	~S V ~P
F T T T	F T **F** F T
T T F F	F T **T** T F
T F F T	T F **T** F T
T F F F	T F **T** T F

When you look under the column of the main operator for both of these statements (marked in bold), you will notice that they have the exact same truth-values on each line. So, these two statements are logically equivalent—De Morgan's Laws. However, look at the following example below:

S • P	~(S • P)
T **T** T	**F** T T T
T **F** F	**T** T F F
F **F** T	**T** F F T
F **F** F	**T** F F F

When you look under the column of the main operator for both of these statements (marked in bold), you will notice that they have the exact opposite truth-values on each line. So, these two statements are contradictory.

Exercise 5.8 continued

5.8.3 *Directions:* Compute the truth-values for the following compound statements. Since you do not have the corresponding truth-values for the simple statements, you must construct a truth table below the compound. Finally, determine if the compound statement is a *tautology*, *self-contradiction*, or *contingent*.

1. [(H • H) ∨ ~H]

*2. D ⊃ ~ T

3. ~(R ≡ ~W) ⊃ W

4. [H • (G ≡ J)] ∨ ~G

5. [(S ∨ R) ∨ (T ⊃ R)] ≡ ~(S ∨ T)

6. ~[[~(B ∨ C) • (A ⊃ ~C)] ≡ [~A ⊃ ~(C ⊃ ~B)]]

3. Testing Validity of Arguments

An argument is said to be invalid if the premises are true and the conclusion is false; otherwise, it is valid. So, when testing arguments, you should look for a line in which the premises are true, and the conclusion is false. If there is such a line, then the argument is invalid by that line. If not, then the argument is valid. Let's take a look at an example used earlier in this book:

If you are a lawyer, then you went to law school.

You went to law school.

Therefore, you are a lawyer.

First, we must put the argument into symbolic notation.

(1) L ⊃ S

(2) S

∴ L

In order to construct a truth table, you must first write it out like a lengthy compound statement. You divide each premise with a forward slash and divide the conclusion with two forward slashes.

L ⊃ S /	S //	L
T T T	T	T
T F F	F	T
F T T	T	F
F T F	F	F

If you notice, line 3 has true premises and a false conclusion. So, the argument is invalid from line 3. You should also recognize that this argument is a formal fallacy as well. It is *affirming the consequent.*

If you are a cat, then you are a mammal.

If you are a mammal, then you are an animal.

Therefore, if you are a cat, then you are an animal.

(1) C ⊃ M

(2) M ⊃ A

∴ C ⊃ A

C ⊃ M /	M ⊃ A //	C ⊃ A
T T T	T T T	T T T
T T T	T F F	T F F
T F F	F T T	T T T
T F F	F T F	T F F
F T T	T T T	F T T
F T T	T F F	F T F
F T F	F T T	F T T
F T F	F T F	F T F

If you notice, there is no line in which the premises are true, and the conclusion is false; thus, the argument is valid. This argument is a pure hypothetical syllogism, which is called the *transitive property* in mathematics.

Exercise 5.9

5.9.1 *Directions:* Determine whether the following arguments are valid or invalid. If it is valid, then write "valid." If the argument is invalid, write "invalid" and put the line that has true premises and a false conclusion.

*1. (1) A ⊃ B

(2) ~A

∴ ~B

2. (1) A ∨ B

(2) A

∴ ~B

3. (1) A ≡ B

(2) A ∨ B

∴ A • B

4. (1) A ⊃ B

(2) C ⊃ B

∴ A ⊃ C

5. (1) A ⊃ B

(2) B ⊃ A

∴ (A • B) ∨ (~A • ~B)

6. (1) [(C ∨ B) ⊃ ~A]

(2) C ⊃ A

∴ B ⊃ ~A

7. (1) A ⊃ (B • C)

(2) ~C

∴ ~A

8. (1) (A ∨ B) ∨ (B ∨ C)

(2) A ∨ C

∴ B ⊃ C

4. Formal Fallacies

As you learned in an earlier section, informal fallacies are problems with the content of the argument. A formal fallacy is a problem with the internal structure of an argument. All formal fallacies are invalid arguments.

All cats are animals.

All dogs are animals.

Therefore, all cats are dogs.

(1) All C are A

(2) All D are A

∴ All C are D

Just because the *C*s are all contained in the *A*s, and the *D*s are contained in the *A*s does not show any relation between the *C*s and the *D*s. It is possible that although both *D*s and *C*s are contained in the *A*s that the *C*s and *D*s are utterly distinct from one another. So, there is at least one interpretation in which the premises are true, and the conclusion is false, and that by definition, is an invalid argument. So, the terms used for *C*, *D*, and *A* are irrelevant when it comes to checking the form. No matter what terms we replace with *C*, *D*, and *A*, the internal structure necessitates that the argument is invalid.

If you are a lawyer, then you went to law school.

You went to law school.

Therefore, you are a lawyer.

(1) $L \supset S$

(2) S

∴ L

A conditional statement expresses the relation between a sufficient condition and a necessary condition. So, the conditional in this argument states that if you have satisfied the sufficient condition, then you must have one of the necessary conditions. Then, the argument says that you have a necessary condition, and you must have the sufficient condition. It should be immediately apparent that the sufficient condition does not follow from one necessary condition, but the converse is true. The name of this formal fallacy is *affirming the consequent*.

Note the similarities between the example above and the following example.

If you are a lawyer, then you went to law school.

You are not a lawyer

Therefore, you did not go to law school.

(1) $L \supset S$

(2) ~L

∴ ~S

This argument is invalid for nearly the same reason as the former. The conditional expresses the relation between a sufficient condition and a necessary condition. Just because you have not satisfied the sufficient condition, does not mean that you have not completed one of the necessary conditions, which is what the argument is expressing. It is possible not to be a lawyer, even though you completed law school. The name of this formal fallacy is called *denying the antecedent.*

Either turn the lights off, or the electric bill will be very high.

I turned all of the lights off.

Therefore, the electric bill will not be very high.

(1) $L \vee B$

(2) L

∴ ~B

In Logic, we use the *inclusive or*. An *inclusive or* is different from the *exclusive or* in a few different respects. An *inclusive or* is one or the other, or both. An *exclusive or* is one or the other, not both. So, if we adopt the *inclusive or* in classical logic, it could be the case that the lights are turned off, and the electric bill is still high (swimming pools consume a ton of energy). By the fact that you have one of the disjuncts does not allow you to infer anything about the other disjunct. For this reason, the following argument is committing a formal fallacy as well.

(1) $L \vee B$

(2) L

∴ B

Both the preceding arguments assert one of the disjuncts in the second premise. From the fact that you have asserted one disjunct does not allow you to infer anything about the other disjunct. So, either B or ~B follows from those premises.

Exercise 5.10

5.10.1 *Directions:* Indicate whether the following statements are true or false.

1. Formal fallacies are based upon issues with the content of the argument.
2. The *actual* truth of the premises determines a formal fallacy.
3. To determine if a formal fallacy has been committed, you must first put the argument into argument form.
4. Classical logic uses the *inclusive or*.
5. All formal fallacies are invalid arguments.
6. All invalid arguments are formal fallacies.
7. Formal fallacies can be spotted by looking at the terms in the original argument.
8. *Affirming the antecedent* is a formal fallacy.

5.10.2 *Directions:* Determine whether the following arguments are committing a formal fallacy. If so, then please write "fallacy" and if not, then please write "No fallacy".

*1. $(P \vee Q) \supset D$

D

$\therefore P \vee Q$

2. $E \vee T$

$\sim T$

$\therefore \sim E$

3. All R are H

All I are H

∴ All R are I

4. $W \supset M$

W

$\therefore M$

5. $(N \bullet C) \supset (S \equiv D)$

$\sim(S \equiv D)$

$\therefore \sim(N \bullet C)$

5. Proofs

As discussed in an earlier section, imagine that you are to pass through a sequence of doors in order to emerge from the final door. You must only move through one door at a time, and in order from the first door to the last. In this process, you will be given a set of four keys. Some of these keys may be used more than once; however, only one key will open each door. So, the quickest and possibly the easiest method to get through the doors is by process of elimination. Test a key, if it does not work, then move onto the next key, until you have made it through the door. The keys that we are using are valid rules of inference. Those keys are *modus ponens, modus tollens, disjunctive syllogism*, and *hypothetical syllogism*. If you are still not clear why these are valid rules of inference, then you may construct a truth table to test the validity for each one. You will find that there is no line in which the premises are true, and the conclusion is false; hence they are valid. Think of these valid rules of inference as entailments to further truths.

Modus Ponens (MP):

(1) $P \supset Q$

(2) P

$\therefore Q$

Modus Tollens (MT):

(1) $P \supset Q$

(2) $\sim Q$

$\therefore \sim P$

Disjunctive Syllogism (DS):

(1) $P \vee Q$

(2) $\sim P$

$\therefore Q$

Hypothetical Syllogism (HS):

(1) $P \supset Q$

(2) $Q \supset R$

$\therefore P \supset R$

Let's complete the following proofs.

(1) G ⊃ ~H	P	//~I
(2) I ⊃ H	P	
(3) G	P	

Here are three premises and a conclusion. The premises are numbered along the left side. The letter *P* denotes the premise(s). Now we should see if one of the four keys will allow us to make a further inference. I can use premise (1) and (3) to perform *modus ponens.*

1	(1) G ⊃ ~H	P	//~I
2	(2) I ⊃ H	P	
3	(3) G	P	
1,3	(4) ~H	1, 3 MP	

Each line depends on other lines. So, we keep track of the dependencies on the left-hand side. Premises (1), (2), and (3) depend on themselves. Line (4) depends upon the truth of the premises (1) and (3), and is the reason that you put those dependencies there. Now that you made it through the first door, you should prepare for the second door.

1	(1) G ⊃ ~H	P	//~I
2	(2) I ⊃ H	P	
3	(3) G	P	
1,3	(4) ~H	1, 3 MP	
1,2,3	(5) ~I	2, 4 MT	QED

The final step is to perform *modus tollens* on lines (2) and (4). Modus ponens allows you to infer ~I, which is the conclusion that we are trying to prove. Let's have a look at another example.

(1) A	P	//C
(2) A ⊃ (C ∨ B)	P	
(3) B ⊃ D	P	
(4) ~D	P	

The first move that should perform is modus ponens on line (1) and (2).

1	(1) A	P	//C
2	(2) A ⊃ (C ∨ B)	P	
3	(3) B ⊃ D	P	
4	(4) ~D	P	
1,2	(5) C ∨ B	1, 2 MP	
3,4	(6) ~B	3, 4 MT	
1,2,3,4	(7) C	5, 6 DS	QED

Exercise 5.11

5.11.1 *Directions:* Complete the following proofs using the four rules of inference: *modus ponens, modus tollens, disjunctive syllogism,* and *hypothetical syllogism.*

1. W ⊃ X //Y
   ~W ⊃ Y
   ~X
2. H ∨ ~G //~J
   G ∨ ~J
   ~H
3. (M • N) ⊃ O //R
   (M • N) ∨ R
   ~O
4. ~F ⊃ ~D //~G
   (~F ⊃ ~E) ⊃ ~G
   ~D ⊃ ~E
5. ~T ⊃ S //R
   ~T ∨ (~S ⊃ R)
   ~S
6. B ⊃ [~C ⊃ (B ⊃ A)] //A
   C ∨ B
   ~C
7. ~W ⊃ [(X ⊃ Y) ⊃ (W ∨ ~Y)] //~X
   ~Z ⊃ Y
   X ⊃ ~Z
   ~W
8. A ∨ (B ∨ C) //C
   D ∨ (B ⊃ D)
   D ∨ ~A
   ~D

9. $(T \vee R) \vee (R \supset S)$ $//M \supset {\sim}N$

   $(T \vee R) \supset ({\sim}Q \equiv {\sim}P)$

   $S \supset {\sim}N$

   $M \supset R$

   ${\sim}({\sim}Q \equiv {\sim}P)$

10. ${\sim}A \supset [(C \supset G) \supset (A \vee {\sim}F)]$ $//{\sim}G$

    $(C \supset F) \supset {\sim}A$

    $C \supset G$

    $G \supset F$

11. $A \supset (B \bullet C)$ $//{\sim}S$

    $(B \bullet C) \supset D$

    ${\sim}D$

12. ${\sim}G \vee (A \supset B)$ $//{\sim}A$

    $(A \supset B) \supset (B \supset {\sim}G)$

    ${\sim}{\sim}G$

13. ${\sim}(S \bullet T)$ $//{\sim}W$

    ${\sim}Q$

    ${\sim}S \supset [S \vee (W \supset Q)]$

    $S \supset (S \bullet T)$

14. $A \supset B$ $//{\sim}D$

    C

    $(A \vee {\sim}D) \supset {\sim}B$

    $C \supset (A \vee {\sim}D)$

15. $G \supset H$ $//{\sim}G$

    $(I \supset H) \supset {\sim}J$

    ${\sim}I \supset [(I \supset G) \supset (K \vee {\sim}H)]$

    $I \supset G$

    ${\sim}K$

Answers to Selected Exercises

Section 2

2.1.2

Objective—A claim is said to be objective, if and only if, it does not depend on an individual to be true. There is a fact of the matter independent of any individual. These are verifiable, measurable, and exist with or without humans. For example, water is H_2O. That is, there are two atoms of hydrogen and one atom of oxygen. This is the case independent of us knowing it.

2.2.3

4. 1. All mammals are animals.

   2. The Saiga antelope is a mammal

   ∴ The Saiga antelope is an animal.

Section 3

3.1.2

2. Being a bachelor is a __sufficient__ condition for being unmarried.

3.1.3

10. If Duchamp's "The Fountain" is considered art, then anything without exception is considered art.

    Conditional Statement

3.2.1

7. At Macomb Community College, 85% of the students who attend earn degrees. Therefore, it is very likely that if you begin your degree, then you will finish it.

    Inductive argument based upon probability

3.3.3

4. I recently purchased a swimming pool for my backyard. The pool is 18′ × 33′ × 4′. Therefore, it must be the case that the pool holds 14,000 gallons of water.

    Deductive argument based upon mathematical calculation. Sound with true premises.

Section 4

4.2.1

7. My European vacation was so amazing and wonderful. Each day was more incredible than the previous day.

    Emotive meaning. You are using emotionally charged language that evokes a positive feeling and thus you have not defended your position.

4.4.2

5. Professor, Peter Singer, Scholar, Human, Man

    Peter Singer, Professor, Scholar, Man, Human

4.5.1

10. "Precisify" means to make a term more precise than it currently is.

    Stipulative definition.[1]

4.6.1

3. You often vote Republican in elections. But you are a business owner, and you will see the immediate benefits of the tax-cuts. Clearly, the only reason that you vote Republican is because you will directly benefit from voting that way.

    Ad hominem circumstantial

4.6.3

1. I used to work for the Federal government. The government does a really good job convincing the people that things are one way, when in fact, things are entirely different. You cannot trust the government at all. Thus, you should not dismiss conspiracy theories as crack-pot theories because they are all true.

    False Dichotomy

4.6.5

6. Millennials are so soft nowadays. Make sure to not let them fall down.

    Equivocation on the word "soft"

Section 5

5.1.2

1. No Bernese mountain dogs are vicious animals.

    Some Bernese mountain dogs are not vicious animals.

---

[1] Wakefield, Bradley. *Trivalency in a Contextual Penumbra: An Alternative Solution to the Sorites Paradox*. Wayne State University, 2014. Print.

5.1.3

1. Some robots are not self-autonomous beings.

   Some robots are self-autonomous beings.

5.1.4

1. No books are newspapers.

   Some books are newspapers.

5.2.1

6. All S are P. ∴ Some S are P.

   Invalid, Existential Fallacy

5.2.2

5. Some skydivers are fearless human beings. Therefore, it is false that all skydivers are fearless human beings.

   The premise is an "I" and the conclusion is an "O." The argument is invalid.

5.3.1

1. "A" is true

   E : F

   I : T

   O : F

5.3.2

1. No musicals are operas. Therefore, it is false that all musicals are operas.

   The premise is an "E" and the conclusion is an "O". The argument is valid since musicals exist.

5.4.1

3. No non-S are non-P. *T* (cont.)

    No P are S. *U*

5.4.3

1. All students are inquisitive learners.

    Therefore, all inquisitive learners are students.

    Invalid, Illicit Conversion

5.5.1

3. No pieces of fictional writing are true stories.

    Therefore, some true stories are not pieces of fictional writing.

1. No P are T (T)	
2. No T are P (T)	Conversion
∴ Some T are not P (T)	Subalternation

5.6.2

1. All pseudo-sciences are a complete waste of time. All holistic approaches to medicine are a complete waste of time. Therefore, all holistic approaches to medicine are pseudo-sciences.

    1. All P are C

    2. All H are C

    ∴ All H are P

5.7.1

13. Drinking a tall glass of iced tea on a hot summer day is a sufficient condition for quenching your thirst.

    $D \supset Q$

5.7.2

10. ~[(T • G) ∨ (T ∨ ~G)] ⊃ (B ≡ ~W)

    WFF

5.8.2

2. L ⊃ N

    T ⊃ F

    F̲

5.8.3

2. D ⊃ ~T

    T F̲ F T

    T T̲ T F

    F T̲ F T

    F T̲ T F   Contingent

5.9.1

1. A ⊃ B / ~A // ~B

    T T T F T̶ F T̶

    T F F F T̶ T F̶

    F T T T F̶ F T̶   Invalid Line 3

    F T F T F̶ T F̶

5.10.2

1. (P ∨ Q) ⊃ D

    D

    ∴ PQ   Affirming the Consequent